John Courtenay, Robert Jephson

Essays from the Batchelor

In Prose and Verse. Vol. II

John Courtenay, Robert Jephson

Essays from the Batchelor
In Prose and Verse. Vol. II

ISBN/EAN: 9783744689281

Printed in Europe, USA, Canada, Australia, Japan

Cover: Foto ©Thomas Meinert / pixelio.de

More available books at **www.hansebooks.com**

ESSAYS

FROM THE

BATCHELOR,

IN

PROSE AND VERSE

By the AUTHORS of the
EPISTLE to GORGES EDMOND HOWARD, ESQ.

IN TWO VOLUMES.

VOL. II.

THE SECOND EDITION, WITH ADDITIONS.

DUBLIN, PRINTED;
LONDON, reprinted, for T. BECKET, in the Strand.
MDCCLXXIII.

THE
BATCHELOR.

NÚMBER XLIV.

To JEOFFRY WAGSTAFFE, Efq.

THE paffionate and tender fentiments of love, are expreffed with elegance and claffical purity, in the following beautiful verfes. By inferting them in your Speculations, you will oblige,

MUSÆUS.

KISSES.

By PAUL JODDEREL, Efq.
SOLICITOR *to the late* PRINCE *of* WALES.

AS erft to Damon's facred fhade,
   Thefe eyes their greatful tribute paid,
Of many a tear beguil'd :
Sweet Anna faw my tender grief,
And in kind pity brought relief :
   She kifs'd me, and I fmiled.

Ambition next my bosom warm'd,
Adieu each softer care :
   Alarm'd the fair enchantress came;
One kiss infus'd a gentler fire,
I felt the nobler heat expire,
   And curs'd the phantom Fame.

Transfix'd by Envy's poison'd dart,
When late my inly-fest'ring heart,
   Consum'd in silent pain ;
Like wounded Edward's gen'rous bride,
Sweet Anne her balmy lips apply'd,
   And drew out all the bane.

Strange to relate, the tygress Rage,
Her gentle kisses can assuage,
   And in soft fetters bind ;
Not music's powerful charms e'er gain'd,
Or calm philosophy attain'd
   Such empire o'er the mind.

Then to secure my peace and bliss,
Sweet Anne, in one eternal kiss,
   Breathe in th' all healing balm ;
No, cease thou fatal fond desire,
Ah, treach'rous kisses, you inspire
   More passions than you calm.

NUMBER XLV.

Pindarum quifquis ftudet æmulari. HOR.

A PINDARIC ODE, *fet to Mufic, and performed at Doctor* LUCAS's *Houfe in Henry-
ftreet, on the Birth of his Daughter.*

I MUST, I will afpire,
　　And wake the fleeping lyre ;
　Fair Libertina's praife to fing :
Celeftial Mufe defcend,
Thy infpiration lend,
　　And bear me on thy tow'ring wing.

Shout, fhout, all Chequer-lane,
Raife high the jocund ftrain,
　　To notes of rapture, fwell thy voice ;
Smock-alley, and Blind-quay,
Exalt the choral lay,
　　Ye fons of Pimlico rejoice !

June to adorn,
This day, a babe is born,
　　The fruit of LUCAS' latter days :
The mother chafte and kind,
With perfevering mind,
　　Long toil'd this patriot plant to raife.

B 2

Beat,

Beat, beat, the thund'ring drums,
She comes, fair Freedom comes,
  Her new born triumphs to difplay ;
The Comb, and Poddle crowd,
Should hail with voices loud,
  Fair Libertina's natal day.

Oh lovely Libertine,
In all thy air and mien,
  I fee bright Liberty portray'd ;
Thy amorous fparkling eye,
Thy lip, thy leg and leper thigh,
  For freedom's rapturous joys are made.

Hark, hark the infant fpeaks,
In infant notes fhe fqueaks,
  " Da, to thy country, ftill be true."
Amaz'd nurfe Phegan cries,
" Sweet mifs, God fave your eyes,
  " And God fave da, and country too."

The cocklofts catch the found,
To kitchen it went round ;
  The fcullion, " Save my country !" cries.
Above ftairs and below,
The patriot accents flow,
  While Libertina freedom fqualls.

Lucas, the fage, the grey,
Charm'd with the found grows gay,

                              And

And of his wond'rous offspring proud,
His crutches he forgoes,
Springs high on chalky toes,
    And " Save my country !" echoes round.
" This happy babe, he cries, I fee,
" In times remote fhall copy me,
    " And vulgar females foar above :
" To fpurn reftraint fhall be her pride,
" Her freedom's voice alone fhall guide,
    " In politics and love.
" Warm'd with Macauly's generous rage,
" Deep read in Wilkes's pious page,
    " This maid, her country fhall reclaim:
" Hibernia's modeft manners taught,
" With all my low'ring fpirit fraught,.
    " I fee, I fee her foar to fame.
" To thee, O Phegan, I confign,
" This miracle, this maid divine ;
    " Let her, her father's triumphs know,
" Tell her whole corporations quake,
" And Vice-roys tremble, when he fpake,
    " While freedoms fons with rapture glow.
" Tell her, when young and poor,
" I kept a fhop obfcure ;
    " My foul afpir'd on daring wings,
" Even glifters when I gave,
" I fpurn'd an impious flave,
    " And libell'd minifters and kings.

" When

" When by a bafe and fervile band,
" The licens'd robbers of the land,
  " To Newgate I was doom'd a prey,
" A patriot firm, I perfever'd,
" Nor long the haughty Commons fear'd,
  " But ftole triumphantly away.

" Thus, when my ftory's told,
" Like me in virtue bold,
  " She'll bravely fcorn each fervile hack :
" By no falfe fhame difmay'd
" Of no man's pow'r afraid,
  " On no man will fhe turn her back.

" Now, Phegan, be the babe convey'd
" To Copper-alley's favoury fhade,
  " To fave her from vile courtier's ire ;
" With brandy ftain her tender lip,
" Oft whifkey's fpirit let her fip,
  " With patriot thoughts her foul to fire.

" In Turnftile-alley's friendly gloom,
" Where fheltered from the glare of noon,
  " The fair are fcreen'd from bailiffs foul,
" Let her, while youthful blood invites,
" Freely indulge love's foft delights,
  " And crown with punch the mantling
    " bowl.

" Oft in her riper years employ,
" Some porter ftrong, or butcher's boy,

" To ftruggle with the growing maid :
" That every mufcle firmly-fet,
" Her body, as her mind, befit,
   " Fair freedom's warlike band to lead.

" In field renown'd of Runymede,
" On copy fair of Magna Charta laid ;
   " Lo puritan Macaulay reft :
" See pious Wilkes curl round the dame,
" Behold fhe mingles flame with flame,
   " And *forty-five* times clafps him to her
      " breaft.

" What glitt'ring vifions charm my eyes !
" What fcenes of future glory rife !
   " From this embrace, *another* Wilkes I fce,
" I fee him doom'd to Libertina's bed,
" I fee (the fcourge of thrones) their iffue
      " fpread ;
   " All hail, illuftrious free-born progeny !"

Thus fpoke the fire, and in his arms
Embraced his daughter's infant charms,
   And dandled her and kifs'd :
Fair Libertina fmil'd and fquall'd,
And playful laugh'd, and playful bawl'd,
   And jump'd, and kick'd, and p——fs'd.

NUMBER XLVI.

Cum tot fuftineas, et tanta negotia folus.   HOR.

An EPISTLE *to* GORGES EDMOND HOWARD, *Efq. with Notes explanatory, critical, and hiftorical, by* GEORGE FAULKNER, *Efq. and* Alderman. *The Ninth Edition, with material Additions.*

Advertifement, by the Annotator.

THIS Poem is juftly ranked with the moft celebrated compofitions of Doctor Swift, Pope, Major Pack, Cowley, Prior, Mrs. Pilkington, Parnel, Addifon, and Henry Jones, whofe Works may be had, bound or in fheets, at my Shop in Parliament-ftreet. I have undertaken, at the requeft of my friends, to add Annotations, Remarks, Strictures, and Obfervations, explanatory, critical, and hiftorical, for the benefit of ftrangers, who might otherwife be ignorant of many perfons, things, and circumftances, alluded to in the compofition, after the manner and form of my Notes on Dr. Jonathan Swift, D. S. P. D. that have not a little contributed to improve, and likewife make his Works be underftood. I fhould now likewife obferve, that it hath already gone thro' eight editions in the city of Dublin, this being the ninth, and two in London, where I am lefs known, but by my Journal

and

and the Earl of Chesterfield which maketh its circulation much more general, the Monthly Reviewers for the month of August 1772, remarking, " That it is a piece of excellent humour at " the expence of Mr. Faulkner the printer," affording the highest entertainment thereat; whereby they mean Mr. Howard the Attorney. Printed by William Goldsmith, in Pater-noster-Row; and T. Lewis, in Ruffel street, Covent-garden.

An EPISTLE to GORGES EDMOND HOWARD, Esq. (a)

LET F-k-r boast (b) of rhymes and letters,
To praise himself and maul his betters;

For

(a) *Epistle to G. E. H.*]—He hath amassed a considerable fortune by various means, and lived in tolerable repute, as a practising attorney; till he quarrelled with the author hereof; who has since exposed him in sundry witty paragraphs, pointed epigrams, stinging repartees, facetious verses, biting epistles, humorous acrostics, sharp railleries, keen retorts, brilliant quibbles, and anonymous stanzas.

(b) *Let Faulkner boast, &c.*]—George Faulkner, printer, bookseller, and author of the Dublin Journal. He hath lived with the first wits of the present age in great credit, and upon a footing of much intimacy and kindness. He is well known to have been the particular friend of the dean of St. Patrick's, and at this moment corresponds with the earl of Chesterfield, whose letters will be pub-

For law and wit we read your page,
Which guides the courts, and charms the
    ſtage (c).

                                  The

---

liſhed by him immediately after the demiſe of ſaid
earl. He was ſent to Newgate by the Houſe of
Commons, in the year 1738, for his ſteadineſs in
prevaricating in the cauſe of liberty; and ſworn
an alderman of Dublin in the year 1770: fined
for not ſerving the office of ſheriff in the year
1768. His Journal (to which he hath lately-added
a fourth column) is circulated all over Europe, and
taken in at the coffee-houſes in Conſtantinople,
beſides Bath, Briſtol, Boſton, Tunbridge Wells,
Brighthelmſtone, Virginia, and Eyre-Connaught.
In his paragraphs he hath always ſtudied the proſ-
perity and honour of his native country, by ſtre-
nuouſly decrying of whiſkey, projecting cellars,
holes made by digging for gravel in the high
roads, voiding of excrements in the public ſtreets,
throwing of ſquibs, crackers, ſky-rockets, and
bone-fires; by which many lives are loſt, men,
women, and children maimed, ſick perſons diſ-
turbed out of their ſleep, eyes burned out, and
horſes ſtartled; recommending it to archbiſhops,
dukes, lords, privy-counſellors, generals, co-
lonels, field-officers, and captains, to fall down
precipices, tumble into cellars, be overturned by
rubbiſh thrown in the ſtreets, in order to remove
nuiſances; diſſuading all bloods, bucks, ſmarts,
rapparees, and other ſuch infernal night-walkers,
from committing man-ſlaughter upon pigs, hackney horſes, watchmen's lanterns, and other enor-
mities: profane curſing and ſwearing, and break-
                                    ing

The *ermin'd fages* quote your *Pleas,*
And children lifp your roundelays.

On

---

ing the Sabbath, and the Commandments; exclaiming againft the importation of potatoes, and
advifing to grow more corn; inciting to virtue by
characters in his Journal, and calling upon the
magiftrates to do their duty.—The earl of Chefterfield compareth him unto Atticus, a Roman ba-
ronet, and fundry other compliments.——N. B.
His nephew Todd, continueth to make the beft
brawn, and hath lately imported a large quantity
of James's Powders.

Befides the great men above-mentioned, as
dean Swift and the earl of Chefterfield, who at
prefent correfpond with the author hereof, he hath
the moft kind, affectionate, and complimentary
letters from the celebrated Mr. Pope, of which
the following underwritten epiftle is a copy.

" To Mr. George Faulkner, Bookfeller, in
" Dublin.

" S I R,

" I hear you have lately publifhed an edition
" of Doctor Swift's Works: fend it to me by the
" firft opportunity, and affure the Dean that I am
" ever, his fincere and affectionate fervant.

" ALEXANDER POPE."

Alfo the following moft friendly letter from the famous Mr. Wilkes.

" To Alderman Faulkner, Dublin.

" S I R,

" As I have no farther occafion for your Jour-
" nal; I defire you will difcontinue fending it to
" your humble fervant,   JOHN WILKES."

Which

On Fancy's wing aloft you foar,
To praife Monroe (*d*), and Letty Gore ;

Their

(*c*) *Which guides the courts, and charms the ftage.*]
—Howard hath publifhed Pleas on the Exchequer
Equity ; Rules of Chancery ; Almeyda, or the
Rival Kings, a Tragedy ; the Siege of Tamar,
and the Female Gamefter in Manufcript.

(*d*) *To praife Monroe.*]—This hinteth unto the
under-written ftanzas of faid Howard, whereby he
advifeth and encourageth a painter to proceed in
painting faid lady, and likewife publicly declareth,
that he himfelf will be an adventurer, and will
dare to undertake to complete, and alfo to finifh
the piece, by partly fupplying fome hints, whereby faid painter may be forwarded in his work.

*To a certain Nobleman, on being told he had wifhed for
the Picture of a celebrated Beauty.*

Fond fwain, I hear your wifh is fuch,
Some painter fhould on canvafs touch
    The beauties of Monroe ;
But where's th' adventurer will dare
The happy mixture to prepare,
    Her peerlefs charms to fhew.

Yet by thofe radiant beauties fir'd,
And my ambitious mufe infpir'd,
    Let me fome hints fupply :
To nature's ftores then ftraight refort,
Cull ev'ry tint, the goddefs court,
    This piece to dignify.

—Firft, let the cheek with blufhes glow,
Juft as when damafk rofes blow,

Glift'ning

Their charms shall last in song divine,
Like embryos preserv'd in wine (e).

Your

Glist'ning with morning dew;
Contrasted with the virgin white,
With which the lily glads the sight,
Blend them in lovely hue.

And truly then, that cheek to grace,
Upon her flowing tresses place
The chesnut's auburn down;
Her lips you may in sort depaint,
By cherries ripe, yet ah 'twere faint,
Should them with her's be shewn.

Next, let two eyes with lustre gleam,
Ev'n as the sun's reflected beam,
Upon the glassy lake;
Tinge it with dye of brilliant jet,
Let it in milk be sweetly set,
Each wand'ring heart to take.

Let the transparent web of lawn,
Be o'er the virgin bosom drawn,
As fair—yet cold as snow;
That love may thro' the veil espy,
What else were more than mortal eye,
Cou'd view and safely know.

But O to trace th' internal grace,
That beams divinely in her face,
How vain the muse would soar:
If e'er celestial cherub came,
To bless thy sight, in mystic dream,
Snatch that—the task is o'er.

(e) *Like embryos preserv'd in wine.*] — Embryos
are young children which are not born, which
anatomists

Your claffic pencil finely traces,
The beauties of the SISTER GRACES ; (f)
                                    When

---

anatomifts, after they come into the world, preferve
in fpirits of wine in bottles.   There is the fineft
collection of thefe in the known world, in the
College Anatomy-houfe, in Dublin ; alfo many
human figures of both fexes in wax, in the fact of
child-bearing, a dead fhark, and an Ægyptian
mummy, as old as king Charlemagne.—It may
be of great fervice to families who are apt to keep
their children in bottles, to mention an accident
which happened by this means, to a perfon who
was my particular acquaintance.   Being taken in
the night with a violent tooth-ach, and wanting
to fwage it with brandy, or fome hot liquor, he
ftarted out of bed in the dark, and feized a bottle
which he found on the top of the chimney, but
being furprifed to meet fomething folid between
his teeth, he cried out to his lady, who was afleep
by his fide, what's this in the bottle over the chimney ? and was much concerned and ready to vomit, when fhe replied, that it could be nothing
elfe but poor little Dickey. — By burying them de-
cently as foon as they are born, it may prevent
their being drank, and other accidents to which
bottled children are liable.

(f) *The beauties of the* SISTER GRACES.]—Three
Mifs Montgomeries, on whom Howard wrote the
following under-written verfes, printed in thefe
notes.

On the Abfence and Return of the THREE
FAVOURITE SISTERS.

Of late Love's Queen all in defpair,
Fled through each region of the air,

When in an eafy vein you tell us,
Of Love's miftake, and Venus jealous.

His fire, his fortune to improve,
To ftudy law young Ovid drove (g),
He heeded nought but verfe and love.

The

Her graces were aftray:
To feek them Maia's winged fon,
From Pole to Pole with fpeed had run;
It was a buftling day.

Cupid, who had to earth been fent,
Return'd, with hafte and toil near fpent,
And vow'd he faw them there:
That 'twas on fam'd Ierne's fhore,
Than which with beauties none fhines more,
On the tereftrial fphere.

Straightway a troop of little Loves,
Who tend their Queen where e'er fhe moves,
And bafk in her fweet eyes:
Flew for the nymphs, whom, when they brought,
Alack! 'twas found the urchins caught,
The three Montgomeries.

Soon as their charms fhone full to view,
The Paphian Goddefs jealous grew,
She fear'd her future reign:
Her boy fhe chid for his miftake,
Nor would forgive, 'till he took back
The three to earth again.

(g) *To ftudy law young Ovid drove.*] — Ovid,
otherwife called Nafo, a famous poet in the reign
of Auguftus. He wrote feveral books of Meta-
morphofis, or the changing of one thing into an
other,

The same thy vein ;—but happier you,
Can make estates and verses too ;
In both you equally succeed,
Resistless when you sing or plead :
Thus by the force of diff'rent arts,
Men lose their lands, and maids their hearts.

    Oh how each breast with rapture glow'd,
At your sublime Pindaric Ode (*h*) ;

                      With

---

other, Love Epistles, and Fast Days : he was not
called to the bar, nor ever practised as an attorney.
For farther particulars see his works, *in Usum
Delphini*, printed and sold by me in Parliament-
street.

    (*h*) *At your sublime Pindaric Ode.*]—Howard
wrote an Ode on his Majesty's Birth-day, which
much resembleth Dryden's on the Feast of Alexander.   I have consulted sundry of the best critics,
judges, and geniuses ; Mr. Dexter, who keepeth
the Four-Courts Marshalsea ; Mr. Kavanagh, attorney at law ; Mr. Croker ; Alderman Emerson,
at the Spinning-Wheel, Castle-street, and others ;
who all assure me they don't think Howard's Ode
superior to Dryden's.   In my own opinion, Dryden's is preferable.—For instance, the following
stanzas equal, if not superior to, any of the afore-
said poet's, or of Swift, Pope, Pindar, Plutarch,
or C. Cibber.

I.

  Celestial maids descend and sing,
  With rapture touch the trembling string ;
  To hail the sun of this auspicious morn,
  On which the Star of Britain's isle was born.

                    II. While

With your applaufe the garden rings (*i*),
When you defcribe the beft of Kings ;
All hearts to loyalty you tune (*k*),
'Till Jacobites turn Whigs in June (*l*) !

Well

II.

While conquerors joy in din of arms,
And fhake the globe with dire alarms,
Great G E O R G E's glory is to be
The beft, the Father of the free.

III.

When Death fha'll blot out every name,
And Time fhall break the trump of Fame :
When tongues fhall ceafe, and worlds confume
Thy fame fhall laft, thy glories bloom.

(*i*) *With your applaufe the Garden rings.*]—The Garden, commonly called the New-Gardens, or Doctor Bartholomew Mofs's Gardens. They were opened in the year 1757, and an hofpital erected for lying-in women. 'Tis an excellent charity, and a ftately edifice.—This note was fent me by an ingenious friend, who defires his name may not be made public.

(*k*) *All hearts to loyalty you tune.*]—The people of Ireland are remarkable for a great deal of loyalty, and thick legs : as proof of this, the Government goes in their coaches every 4th of November round the ftatue of his Majefty King George II. at Stephen's-green, in honour of King William III. who hath one of his own in College-green, of glorious and immortal memory, whom God long preferve.

(*l*) *Jacobites turn Whigs in June.*]—The furious, blind, rank fticklers for the houfe of Stuart, were

called

Well Bart'lemon (*m*), you may take pride in
A bard who foars above old Dryden (*n*) ;

For

---

called Jacobites, becaufe they abhorred, detefted,
and difliked King William IIId. of glorious and
immortal memory. I knew a Jacobite of great
learning, parts, and erudition, who was found fmo-
thered alive in the Black-hole at Calcutta, with my
Journal in his fob.

(*m*) *Bart'lemon.*]—A celebrated mufician, who
playeth upon the fiddle at the New-Gardens, or
Doctor Bartholomew Mofs's Gardens. He fet
Howard's Ode to mufic, on the birth-day of his
Majefty George III. whom God long preferve.

Vivat Rex.

(*n*) *A bard who foars above old Dryden.*]—John
Dryden, a poet, who was well known in the reign
of Charles II. He was born of a gentleman's family in Northamptonfhire. In order to give his
countrymen of Ireland fome more intimate knowledge of him, (no author's works having a better
fale at my fhop in Parliament-ftreet) I undertook a
journey to London, to collect materials for his life ;
but after remaining there three months for this purpofe, I could only learn that he was accuftomed
to fit in a big chair among the wits at Button's ;
and this my friends telling me not being fufficient
for a life of faid poet, I accordingly difcontinued
it.

I alfo begun a life of the Dean of St. Patrick's,
in a ftyle which was much admired, and equal to
the fine fimplicity of the Greeks, and the Dean
himfelf, which I begun in this manner. " Dean
" Swift was a man who had wax in his ears." I

am

For who that Howard's Ode can tafte,
Will relifh Alexander's Feaft?
Shou'd foolifh George attempt to turn all
Your works to burlefque, in his Journal,
You'll make him of your wit the butt,
And prove a deadlier foe than Foote (*o*).

For

---

am in poffeffion of many other anecdotes, known
to no perfon now living, and when they are completed it will be publifhed by me and my execu-
tors in Parliament-ftreet.

(*o*) *And prove a deadlier foe than Foote.*]—Samuel
Foote, Efq. manager of the Theatre-Royal in the
Hay-Market, London.   He expofed Alderman
Faulkner, under the character of Peter Paragraph,
in one of his pieces, acted upon Smock-alley ftage,
in Dublin.   He was profecuted for faid offence by
Mr. Faulkner, and tried before Mr. Juftice Robin-
fon, who inveighed very eloquently againft ftage-
players, and faid he might be confidered as rub-
bifh or a dunghill, and brought under the head of
nuifances.—The learned council for the profe-
cutor, alfo compared him unto Ariftophanes, and
the alderman unto Socrates; adding alfo, that
Socrates was not the worfe for the comparifon.
The play-houfe would have run with blood on this
occafion, and many fwords would have been
drawn, had not Mr. Faulkner prevailed on his
friends (who were prefent every night of the re-
prefentation) to hear the piece out, and let him
take his remedy by law; to which they very oblig-
ingly confented.——N. B. Said Foote hath with
impu-

For tho' good-natur'd all your life,
Averse to calumny and strife,
Yet Satire's sting you can impart,
Tho' oft good nature hides the dart :
On thistles thus soft down we spy,
Yet underneath sharp prickles lie ;
In vain the Freeman aid shall bring,
" You're not a bee without a sting (*p*) ;"

Tho'

---

impunity exposed upon the stage, some of the
greatest men, and greatest wits now living; such
as the late Duke of Newcastle, Mr. Glover, the
late Alderman Beckford, Mr. Langford the auc-
tioneer, Mr. Peter Taylor, and the Rev. Mr.
Whitfield. He lost his leg by a providential fall
from his horse, in company with his late Royal
Highness the Duke of York, at the seat of the
Earl of Mexborough, he was taken up much
bruised, and the amputation was performed by
surgeon Bromfeild.

(*p*) " *You're not a bee without a sting.*"]—There
is a peculiar felicity (as I am told) in this compari-
son of Howard unto a bee, although the Epistle
sayeth that he " is not a bee," for whereas a bee
never resteth upon any bud or flower, but flyeth
about in wandring and uncertain angles, from
shrub to shrub, and from hollyhock to poppy,
and never is content until his bags be filled; so
Howard hath amassed an ample fortune by different occupations; and also hath completed a
volume of apophthegms, from the divers rich spoils

Tho' wifely ev'ry fweet you cull,
Of which your apophthegms are full (q).
Your verfe the Irifh (r) SHAMROCK faves,
You ftamp your genius on its leaves :

St.

---

of learning which he hath happened to encounter in his poring over books, many of which he hath had accefs to in my fhop in Parliament-ftreet.

(q) *Of which your apophthegms are full.*]— Some of the greateft geniufes of antiquity, and the moderns, have taken particular delight in collecting all the wife fayings, and brilliant proverbs of the cute obfervers upon men, manners, and things— an excellent collection of this fort is to be found in one of the laft pages of Boyer's French Gentleman's Grammar. But I am informed that the Lord Bacon, Baron Verulam, Vifcount St. Alban's, and Plutarch, have been more induftrious in this way than any of their cotemporaries, the moderns. Howard in imitation of thefe fupernatural wits, is alfo the author of a compilation of an octavo volume, under the title of Howard's Apophthegms, collected from Bacon, Plutarch, Sir John Fielding, Julius Cæfar, the Wit's Vade Mecum, Solon, a Chriftmas Box for Young Ladies, Taylor's Holy Living and Dying, and the Buck's Companion.

(r) *Your verfe the Irifh* SHAMROCK *faves.*]—— This moft certainly meaneth the multifarious collection of poems, printed in a thick volume in quarto, at the inftigation of Mr. White, the writing-mafter, in Grafton-ftreet, by fubfcription, for his benefit, which confifteth of his pupils,
their

St. Patrick with a gracious smile,
Beholds *the* poet of his isle,

In

---

their fathers, grand-mothers, aunts, parents, cousins and other kindred, whose names are made public for the encouragement of the work.——Said Mr. White farther teacheth, and instructeth, young masters, misses, and other children who are come to their full growth, in the Whole Circle of the Sciences, such as Salmon's Gazetteer, astronomy, the whole secret of spelling made easy to the meanest capacities, the use of their letters to those who cannot read, geography, the true meaning of the globes, history, and other branches of the mathematics.——The big book of Madrigals which he published he styleth the SHAMROCK, it being composed of the choicest pieces of wit and humour which ever appeared, and doth great honour to the geniuses of this kingdom, it having been wrote altogether by Irishmen, ladies, and other lords of quality since the Revolution.——Here followeth two of the most admired verses in the whole production, one being An Epigram on "a lady employed in the office of blowing a *turf* fire with her pettycoat, for want of a pair of bellows."——And the other on said lady, "who was so disastrous as to spill a dish of tea upon her apron." Which will do for a sample of the rest, they being equal, if not superior, to any of the foregoing, or those inserted after.

EPI-

In buſkin'd dignity you ſhine,
And prove your claim to Norfolk's *line* (s) ;

That

EPIGRAM. *On a Cup of Tea, ſpilt in a Lady's Lap.*

Mourn nót, AMIRA, that to love's abode
The warm adventurous ſtream preſum'd to preſs :
  Not chance, but ſome unſeen admiring God,
In rapturous ardour, ſought the ſweet receſs.
  Nor doubt what Deity, ſo greatly bold,
In form unuſual thus ſhould viſit théé ;
  The God who raviſh'd in a ſhow'r of gold,
Can charm the *fair* one in IMPERIAL TEA !

EPIGRAM.   *To a young Lady blowing a Turf Fire
with her Petticoat,*

Ceaſe, ceaſe, AMIRA, peerleſs maid !
    Though we delighted gaze,
  While artleſs you excite the flame
    We periſh in the blaze.

  Haply you too provoke *your harm,*
    Forgive the bold remark,
  Your petticoat may fan the fire,
    But, O ! beware a SPARK.

  In the ſame ſtyle and form, and I think more
ſtinging, I made an Epigram on my Nephew
Tom Todd, (which Mr. White promiſeth to in-
ſert in his next edition of the Shamrock) who is
always ſtirring and rooting the fire becauſe he
thinks he can never be hot enough ſince he
was ſun-burnt in the Eaſt-Indies, it being there
dog-days all the year over, ſummer and winter, as
it is with us in the dog-days in Auguſt.——Tom
Todd, ſays I, extempore, You put me to a great
ſupernumerary expence in COALS, which coſts me
a great

That *line* which pull'd *fanatics* down,
And always prop'd the church and crown (7).

                                         You
_____

a great deal of COLE.——COLE is a cant word
among my news-boys and other black-guards,
for cafh, pounds, fhillings, pence, and farthings.
This I have briefly expreffed in my excellent
Epigram, which is as followeth :

   Tom Todd the fire always prokes,
     For he's a hearty foul ;
   His uncle cannot SLACK his jokes,
     But always pays the COLE.

   Mr. Howard was very much enraged becaufe
Mr. White did not print fome of his anagrams
and acroftics in the body of the work, though he
had no juft pretenfion thereto, he not having been
one of Mr. White's pupils, nor a fubfcriber to his
book, who, to pacify his rage, made an Appendix
to make room for him.—N. B. The SHAMROCK
is a green herb, which groweth and flourifheth
among the grafs, in our pleafure-gardens and in
the open fields on St. Patrick's birth day, which
commonly happeneth on the 17th day of March,
and is worn by moft people at home and abroad,
efpecially at court, in croffes in honour of the
Saint, who was the firft chriftian bifhop of Armagh, and converted the poor infatuated natives
of this country from the errors of the church of
Rome, by the help of the Shamrock, as faid White
obferveth.—He likewife banifhed toads, ferpents,
frogs, fnakes, wolves, bears, nightingales, and
other venomous creatures, but was pleafed to
leave us crabs, lobfters, rabbits, and other fea fowl.
—The common people moft commonly get drunk
                                         on

You prove what riches tillage yields (*u*),
And fmiling plenty crowns our fields;

Sure

---

on this day with whifkey, which occafioneth
much fighting, quarrelling, maiming, bruifing,
bad language, and other accidents.

(*s*) *And prove your claim to Norfolk's line.*]—The
Duke of Norfolk's name is Howard, from which
Gorges Howard is defcended in a ftraight line,
his anceftor being the Hon. Mr. Edward Howard,
who was alfo reputed a great dunce in the reign
of King Charles the IId. and compofed feveral
plays and tragedies, fuch as the Britifh Princes,
King Arthur, &c. which fuffered much abufe
and provocation, from the witty noblemen of the
day, being the Earl of Dorfet, Mr. Dryden,
Lord Rochefter, Mr. Butler author of Hudibras,
the Duke of Buckingham and, others.

(*t*) *And always prop'd the church and crown.*]—
Mr. Howard is church-warden of Mary's church,
and was employed as an attorney by the Rev. Mr.
Mofes Magill, the curate of the parifh, to fpeak
againft the Prefbyterians, who refufed to pay faid
Mofes for difturbing them with prayers early in
the morning at an unfeafonable hour, though
they never attended divine fervice; which Mr.
Howard did, to the univerfal fatisfaction of all his
parifhioners at a veftry.—He is likewife folicitor to
the crown, for the quit rents, cafual revenue, and
other forfeited eftates.

(*u*) *You prove what riches tillage yields.*]—Howard
is the author of feveral letters, figned Agricola,
recommended tillage. I printed them without

Sure all who read you muſt allow,
You write as if you held the plough.
You prove by ploughs the kingdom's fed (w),
That *pictures* cannot ſerve for *bread*:
From whence 'tis plain this lazy nation,
Owes to your pen its preſervation.

My muſe the Architect now greets,
Whoſe lofty domes adorn our ſtreets (x) ;

Who,

---

any expence to the author, before our quarrel,
but have ſince declined it. He hath taken moſt
of his hints from my paragraphs, and endeavoured
to imitate my ſtyle and ſpirit; but my friends tell
me he hath failed therein.

(w) *You prove by ploughs the kingdom's fed.*]——
Ploughs, an inſtrument for turning up the earth,
were firſt invented by Triptolemus, a near relation
of the Goddeſs Ceres, and afterwards much im-
proved by Mr. John Wynne, Baker, of the
Dublin Society—The Iriſh formerly ploughed by
the tail with their bullocks; but upon Dr. Swift's
voyage to the Houynhams being publiſhed, and
his ſaying ſo much in praiſe of horſes, this
barbarous, horrid, atrocious, ſhocking, deteſt-
able, cruel, nefarious cuſtom was aboliſhed by act
of parliament. See an Abridgement of the Iriſh
Statutes, ſold by me in Parliament-ſtreet.

(x) *Whoſe lofty domes adorn our ſtreets.*]—Howard owneth many houſes in Parliament-ſtreet. I
built my own houſe myſelf, Howard having nothing to ſay it, nor ſhall ever come within my
doors,

Who, Vanbrugh like, claims double bays (y),
For piling ſtones and writings plays,

Your

---

doors, unleſs it be to pay for advertiſements in my
Journal, or to buy medicines of my nephew Todd.
—It may be worth while to mention a very entertaining anecdote (for the ſatisfaction of the
curious) relating thereunto: when my houſe was
building, I happened to be out of the way one
morning, penning an advertiſement for an agreeable companion to pay half the expence of a poſt-
chaiſe, to ſee that ſtupendous curioſity of nature,
the Giant's Cauſeway, about which 'tis ſtill a doubt
amongſt the learned, whether it be done in the
common way by Giants, or whether it be an effort of ſpontaneous nature, and my houſe was
erected without any ſtair-caſe; whereby the upper
ſtories were rendered uſeleſs, unleſs by the communication of a ladder placed in the ſtreet. But
upon conſidering my misfortune in wanting my
member, and the careleſneſs of hackney coach-
men, who drive furiouſly through the ſtreets at
all hours, in a ſtate of drunkenneſs from the ſpiri-
tuous liquors, whereby the ladder might be ſhook
or thrown down when I was aſcending it, I
thought it better to re-build my houſe, and it has
at preſent a ſtair-caſe, by which there is a convenient and elegant communication between all
parts of ſaid tenement.—It is ſomewhat remarkable that my houſe in Eſſex-ſtreet had no ſtair-caſe,
whereby nature ſeemeth to point out, that having
but one leg, I ought not to attempt climbing, and
ſhould always remain on the ground floor.

(y) *Who, Vanburgh like, &c.*]——Sir John Vanbrugh,

Your skill instructs Gymnastic schools (z),
And Carte and Tierce reduc'd to rules,
Prove you the first of moral men,
To poise a sword, or point a pen.

---

burgh. He was a great poet and architect. I was
not personally acquainted with him any farther
than printing his works, because he died before
my time. Being imprisoned in the Bastile, and
having no light, nor pen or ink allowed him, he
amused himself with drawing divers plans of the
Bastile, which he hath since introduced into many
buildings with great success, particularly Blen-
heim, which much resembleth the Bastile.

(z) *Your skill instructs Gymnastic schools*]——
Howard wrote a treatise on fencing, and is accounted an expert swordsman——He declined
accepting a challenge which I sent him to fight my
nephew Todd, (in the way of proxy) at the Fifteen
Acres, with pistols. I could not fight myself,
because I am pledged to the public for my Journal,
three times a week, and have the care of the city
upon me in my capacity of an alderman. My
nephew was at first unwilling to accept the com-
bat, but upon my promising to leave him the
Journal after my death, and making him take
two spoonfuls of his own *Elixir Vitæ*, he at last
consented. This medicine is only imported by
him, and is excellent for preventing accidents by
sudden death and megrims: It also cureth all
mortal wounds, by gun-shot and other missive
weapons.

New

New light on ev'ry art you ſtrike,
And matchleſs ſhine in all alike;
For who can tell if moſt you're ſkill'd in
The pen, the plough, the ſword, or building?
A puny author may diſcloſe
Some ſkill in rhyme, but none in proſe;
In proſe another ſhews his wit,
Who can't a ſingle ſtanza hit:
Your foes unwillingly confeſs,
In both you equal ſkill poſſeſs (a).

On·

(a) *In both you equal ſkill poſſeſs.*]—This, I conceive alludeth to the following under-written letter
of Mr. Howard's, from Killarney, with the ſig-
nature of POBLICOLA, with a deſcription, and like-
wiſe a compariſon of the Giants Cauſway, whereunto
he ſubjoined an inſcription for the tomb-ſtone of
Dr. Averel, biſhop of Limerick, and uncle to the
right hon. Francis Andrews, Provoſt of Trinity
College, Dublin, that repreſenteth the loyal city of
Londonderry in parliament:—N. B. That Killarney
is a ſmall village of that name in the county of Kerry.
It is a market-town, but doth not ſend two members to parliament, as moſt other boroughs do. It is
part of the eſtate of Lord Viſcount Kenmare, who
hath forfeited his title, he being a Catholic nobleman, although very hoſpitable, and keepeth a
moſt plentiful table, furniſhed with all the va-
rieties the ſeaſon affords. I alſo had the honour
to dine with him when I journeyed into theſe
parts, to ſee the beatuies of this wonderous lake.

On a *true* mirrour's polifh'd face,
All objects thus we plainly trace, ,

But

To the Printer of the DUBLIN MERCURY.

SIR, Killarney, Sept, 26th 1771.

I have at length feen what I have long wifhed
to fee, this wonderous lake. To attempt to defcribe
it would require the ableft pen of the ancient poets,
or, of modern poets, the famous painter of Killarney, wherefore, I fhall never attempt it :——
yet notwithftanding all the beauties of the lake, I
cannot think it, as a curiofity, equal to the
Giants Caufeway; I have feen both. I never faw
any thing LIKE the firft, nor any thing EQUAL
to the latter; this diftinction is agreed to by all
I have mentioned it to. But alas! this lake has
been the death of a man, for whom the whole
province here is in tears, the late bifhop of Limerick, Dr. Averel, our countryman :—To fum up
all fhortly as I can, I heard the people of Limerick,
(where I was fhortly after his death) fay, that there
has not been fuch a bifhop fince the time of
the apoftles; that the Romifh clergy faid, they
fhould not wonder, had he lived any time, if they
had loft many of their flocks.—What obligations
then are due to our Lord Lieutenant, for having
appointed fuch a man their paftor; for though
Heaven has pleafed to take him away, his fuccef-
fors will hear fo much of him, that he cannot but
endeavour to intimate him. I heard this acknowledged by feveral, as alfo for his concurrence in
appointing that well known friend to his country,

and

But if in fpots the MERCU'RY lie,
A broken image meets the eye.

                        O Howard !

---

and their city, efpecially, fpeaker: from thefe and
many other like inftances of his impartial conduct,
it is wifhed that we may never lofe him,——and
every day the advantage of a refident Vice-roy
becomes more and more manifeft ; that from this
new mode of government, there is far more likeli-
hood that merit will be rewarded, proper perfons
appointed to offices, and and the laws fupported
and executed.   A gentleman of our city happen-
ing to be at Limerick, fhortly after the interment
of the bifhop, and hearing the prodigious great
character of him from all perfons, wrote the following lines, extempore, as an infcription for a
monument.

                        POBLICOLA.

Beneath this marble ftone weep, mankind weep,
Averel, your friend, lies wrapp'd in endlefs fleep;
Who, for the poor alone, did fortune crave,
And deem'd himfelf but rich in that he gave ;
From whom, the pray'r of want, or plaint of woe
Ne'er did unpitied, or unhappy go.
His mournful flock to their blefs'd paftor's praife,
With greatful heart this parting tribute pays.

   Before our quarrel, Howard wrote the following
Epitaph on me, which had we continued friends,
I fhould not have been forry to fee put upon my
tomb-ftone, which I now accordingly publifh, that
my friends may fee what an opinion Howard once
entertained of me.

O Howard ! is it not furprizing,
Your wit alone fhould ftop your rifing !
Elfe on the bench you might be thruft,
Tho' flow as fnail, that crawls thro' duft ;
By felf-conceit you might advance,
As quickfilver makes puddings dance (*b*).
From men of fenfe fools win the day,
As horfes fly, when affes bray.

An Epitaph on GEORGE FAULKNER.

Beneath this Stone lyes fet
An Earthly Light,
GEORGE FAULKNER.
To tell you what he was
Would be to tell the World
There was a Sun and Moon.

Oh then
But from this Star
Such Rays divine diverg'd,
Hofpitality, Friendfhip, Love,
That all who faw, admir'd.
Can more be faid ?
If ought,
Say it who can.

(*b*) *As quickfilver makes puddings dance.*]—Nothing is more entertaining to a large company, than to fee a pudding vibrating, fhaking, moving, and dancing upon the difh, by means of quickfilver inferted into the body of it.

O fons

O fons of dulnefs! blefs'd by fate!
Fitteft for law, for church, and ftate;
Your parents influence prevails,
And gives her dunces—mitres—feals:
A Tifdall's depth (c), a Townfhend's wit,
Is not for plodding bufinefs fit:
An Eagle's wings were form'd for flight.
A Goofe's furnifh quills—to write.

I'd alfo fing, if I were able,
Your genrous wine, and feftive table;
Where all thofe wits in crowds affemble;
Who make the vile Committee tremble;
There, Donough's humour mirth provokes (d),
While all admire his *Attic* jokes (e),

Tho.

(c) *A Tifdall's depth.*]—The right hon. Philip Tifdall, Attorney-general.

(d) *There Donough's humour mirth provokes.*]——
The rev. Doctor Dennis, chaplain to the Lord Lieutenant of Ireland; author of many ingenious pieces.

(e) *While all admire his Attic jokes.*]——The people of Attica were remarkable for the goodnefs of their jokes, and for having the beft falt for pre-ferving meat for foreign importation; by which means they underfold all their neighbours in the article of falt provifions. I hope this may be a

C 5

tiuely;

Tho' oft to prove his tafte the beft,
He laughs alone at his own jeft:
Then boafts how once his patron rofe,
And told the ftory of THREE CROWS;
Which he'll infert, with meet apology,
In his new Syftem of Chronology (*f*);
And after mending Newton's errors (*g*),
St. Audeon's-Arch he'll fill with terrors.
The Caftle tribe aloud confefs (*h*)
Him great Alcides of the prefs,
Like that immortal hero known,
For fathering labours *not his own.*

---

timely warning to this poor, undone, infatuated country—Attica was called the Corke of Greece.

(*f*) *In his new Syftem of Chronology.*]——Doctor Dennis is at prefent engaged in digefting a new fyftem of Chronology, under the title of Chronological and Hiftorical Differtations; which I fhall be glad to print and fell at my fhop in Parliament-ftreet.

(*g*) *And after mending Newton's errors.*]——Sir Ifaac Newton. He was made a knight by Queen Anne, and mafter of the mint, a place worth 1000l. yearly. He was reckoned a good mathematician, and was very fond of looking through fpy glaffes.

(*h*) *The Caftle tribe aloud confefs.*]—This alludeth to the Doctor's being the fuppofed author of all the political pieces which appear in the Mercury.

B——w——s,

B——w——s, in epigram fo fmart (*i*),
'Till griping H——rt——d broke his heart (*k*),

Now

(*i*) The Reverend Doctor Lewis Burrows, Curate of St. Thomas's Dublin. He was bred a Sizer or Servitor, in the College of Dublin, and diftinguifhed himfelf very much by his early difpofition to write verfes, which appeared by his infcribing epigrams on moft of the Fellows trenchers, which he had an opportunity of handling after they had dined thereon. When he was too much hurried to conclude an epigram, which happened fometimes by the variety of his occupation, in taking away the cloth, knives, fpoons, forks and other eatables, he always filled up what was wanting in verfe by the figure of a goofe, a gander, or gofling, or fome other emblematic type or fhadow, expreffive of his difpofition for fatire. Being very poor and having no livelihood, he advertifed himfelf as a private tutor, to inftruct youth in morality, religion, geography, law, phyfic, natural philofophy, botany and the globes, at ten pounds per annum. Being taken into a gentleman's family on thefe terms, he was much captivated by the beauty of a young lady who was fifter to his pupil, and by the comelinefs of his perfon, being a fleek man, and remarkably polite in his cloathing, he made fuch a way in this young lady's affections, whofe fortune was in her own power, that he foon made a conqueft of her perfon; but being alfo a man of great prudence, in which he was certainly very commendable, he left her to make the beft of her own folly, thereby conveying

C 6

a very

Now deals in Hebrew roots profound,
And only treads prophetic ground;

Jerus'lem

---

a very useful lesson to all frail young women, and
which he has often said he hopes (being the sole
reason of his doing it) will be a timely warning to
prevent other ladies from falling into such snares.
He afterwards was preferred to a small living in
the diocese of Derry, where he carried on the
Protestant religion with so much zeal against Pa-
pists, especially of the church of Scotland, that he
suffered divers persecutions in consequence thereof,
which he bore with the true meekness of a Christian clergyman, being often kicked, cudgelled,
bruised, tweaked by the nose, and otherwise insulted, which he bore with great humility and
patience.   Hearing a great character of the Earl
of Hertford's administration, as remarkable for
facts, homilies, penitence and true religion, he
proposed himself to his Excellency to write epigrams, to support him against Mr. Flood, Brownlow, &c. who were seldom seen at church, which
he did with great spirit and success, calling them
geese, ganders, goslings, asses, and other oppro-
brious fowl and birds, in the Mercury.   He was
so persecuted for his witty allusions, that he found
it necessary to publish an advertisement in my
Journal, April 24, 1770, swearing thereby on the
faith of a Christian clergyman, that he had no
concern, and never was the author of any production in said paper, and much blaming the
printer Hoey, and another gentleman, for dif-
covering that the letter X in said paper, was his
property,

Jerus'lem artichoke supplies,
Those visions that made Daniel wise..

The

---

property, and that he was the author of many productions therein, which base conduct on their
parts he resented so highly in this impudent in-
decent manner, proving a Christian clergyman a -
liar to the ruin of his character, and the great .
scandal of his holy function, that it determined
him to write in the Freeman's Journal without the
letter X, and as seldom as possible to mention
ganders, geese, and goslings. Soon after he went
into the North, where he was taken into the confidence of a gentleman of great sense and fortune,.
who had near lost his understanding by age and
infirmities, and by the many spiritual comforts he
administered to him, pretending to be a good
Jacobite, and an old Tory; in that condition he
prevailed on him to suppress all ties of blood and
alliance, and bequeath his fortune to a stranger,
instead of three very deserving daughters and their
issue, who were disinherited. The Doctor's true
reason for this was not to make himself necessary
to the heir for the sake of the legacy which was
left him, but for the honour of the church, shew-
ing it is necessary to pay them respect in all families, and that though a Christian clergyman may
be tweaked by the nose, kicked, cuffed, and buf-
fetted, yet the church shall abide, and the gates
of hell shall not prevail against it. He hath the
happy art of persuading old ladies who do not
think of their souls till they are in the other world,
to leave legacies in his hands for the poor, which
he

The Doctor proves to all the nation,
No myst'ry's couch'd in Revelation.
'Till every goffip can explain,   .
What fage divines explore in vain.

No

---

he applieth to the best purpofes, making himfelf
and family, otherwife poor and diftreffed, in a
comfortable way thereby, until he is called upon
in a public manner, to the fcandal of the church,
when he produceth receipts figned after the complaints from which his exemplary life and conduct
as heretofore mentioned, taketh away all colour.
His great genius for poetry, has not only appeared
in his preaching a fermon on the fineft text in
Exodus, chap. xxxii. v. 23. on Chriftmas-day,
" I will take away mine hand and thou fhalt fee
" my back parts, but my face fhall not be feen ;"
but alfo by writing birth-day odes, in the manner
of Mr. Victor, at the moderate price of half a
guinea, poetry and ftationary ware included   He
hath a peculiar faculty for witty epigrams: I have
felected a few as a fpecimen of the Doctor's abilities:

What! fweet Mifs Meredith of Chefter,
    Efpous'd to Alderman Trecothic!
That ftupid cit—but what poffefs'd her,
    To chufe an animal fo Gothic:

Some demon fure her mind mifled,
    To make a choice fo void of reafon;
Elfe what could tempt the girl to wed,
    A wretch who foon muft fwing for treafon.

X.

No juggler ever play'd fuch tricks,
As he with John's feven candlefticks,
By whofe myfterious lights are fpy'd,
Wicklow's Seven Churches typiy'd.

Next

Batchelor Vol. i. Page 62.

A goofe in the oven! no, fir, 'tis a flander,
　As fome, who difcover'd the fact can declare,
For it was not a *goofe*, but you a poor *gander*,
　(As fools will be peeping) who thruft your head
　　there.　　　　　　　　　　　　　　X.

Batchelor No. 25, Vol. i. Page 105.

The great Doctor Phlogos has publifhed an order
That Counfellor Goflin fhall be our Recorder.
　　　　　　　　　　　　　　X.

An Epigram on reading the above.

We're threatned by Phlogos with an action of
　flander,
For calling his fav'rite the fon of a Gander;
In anfwer to which we fhall plead no excufe,
But fhew that the Doctor himfelf is a Goofe:
So he and the Goflin, as birds of a feather,
May both, when they pleafe, bring their actions
　　together.　　　　　　　　　　　X.

Another punifhment propofed for the Gander.

　Heigh ho! that wicked bird produce
　The Gander that defamed the Goofe.　　X.

Another

Next maudlin B———ke (*l*), whofe novels
    pleafe,
Like fome old dotard's reveries,
Without beginning, middle, ending,.
To. *utile* or *dulce* tending,

                                    With:

Another Epigram.

How fhall we ufe the wicked Gander,
That goes about retailing flander ?
Why, fince in fcandal he delights,
Let him read all that Phlogos writes.   X.

(*k*) *'Till griping H—rt—d broke his heart.*]—
Some of my moft familiar and intimate critics and
geniufes is of opinion, that the poet meaneth grip-
ping Hertford, and that it ought therefore to be
fpelled with a double pp.   But I candidly and totally differ from them, and profecute my own opinion, in maintaining. that it implieth, that his
Excellency the faid earl of Hertford, was griev-
oufly afflicted with various diforders of the gripes,.
brought upon him by windy flatulencies, mortal
dry belly-achs, and other pinching ficknefles of the
guts, during. the time he prefided over the chief
government of this his native country ; and that
this was the whole tote of his cafe is notorioufly
known to every human creature, man, woman, or
children, whether in the Caftle,. in the city, or
the fuburbs of Dublin.

    (*l*) *Next maudlin B—ke, &c.*]—Henry Brooke,.
Efq. an excellent poet, philofopher, and patriot.
He hath for fome time retired to his country feat
in the Bog of. Allen, where he is carrying on great
                                    improve-

With equal art, his genius pliant
Can drain a bog, or *quell a giant*.
Whilst one hand wounds each venal brother,
He for a bribe extends the other.
Your character's worth just so much,
As you afford, and he can touch:
With ev'ry virtue he abounds,
Who tips the patriot fifty pounds;

Gold

improvements, in laying the country under water, and searching for hidden treasures in the bottom of lakes, ponds, marshes, sloughs, and other navigable rivers. He published a famous Novel, called, The Fool of Quality, which is sold in separate volumes, or together, at my shop in Parliament-street. There is so much variety in this piece, that the best judges agree, 'tis indifferent at what part you begin to read it, being beautifully interspersed with stories of beggars, trouts, foreign birds, and Indian princesses. The earl of Chesterfield, as a proof of his esteem for his fine talents, made him a barrack-master. He is a true friend to the religion of his country, and hath written many excellent tracts in defence of Popery and the Protestant persuasion. He wrote a ballad opera, called, Jack the Giant Queller, being a satire upon the Lords Justices of Ireland, which was accordingly forbid to be represented. The excellent tragedy of Gustavus was also stopped for the same reason, by the Lord Chamberlain, being a noble incitement to sedition, in the cause of liberty. He

was

Gold works ftrange wonders in his eyes,
Makes cowards brave, and dunces wife.
Like Swifs, his hireling mufe engages,
On any fide that pays beft wages ;
One while ftaunch friend to Martin Luther(*m*),
He finds pure light and gofpel truth there ;

Then

---

was at firft the conductor of the Free Prefs, which truft he executed with great integrity, taking divers fums of money from feveral public officers, to prevent their being fatirized in faid Journal ; which he did with great integrity. This Journal is not fo univerfally circulated and admired as mine, becaufe it containeth not fuch a variety of interefting particulars, intelligence from foreign courts, the Tranfit of Venus, high-water at Dublin-bar, affize of bread, failing and return of packets, births, deaths, and marriages ; not to mention curious queries, and ingenious paragraphs.

(*m*) *One while ftaunch friend to Martin Luther.*]—
A Roman Catholic Clergyman, efteemed a good Preacher. He underftood Italian, French and other languages. He quarrelled with the Pope of Rome about Tranfubftantiation and other church ceremonies. Henry the VIIIth offered him the united bifhopricks of Clonfert and Kilmacduagh, in the county of Galway, which he politely refufed, and publifhed a virulent libel againft faid King. Said King replied with much wit and humour, for which the Pope prefented him a fine Provence Rofe for a Nofegay, and called him Defender of the Faith, and fo forth.—Nicholas Luther,

Then thro' the realm makes proclamation,
For Pop'ry, Priefts, and Toleration.
He firft with many a fair pretence,
To public fpirit, truth, and fenfe,
Hatch'd that difgrace to law and reafon,
That mafs of flander, dullnefs, treafon ;
That Journal which the Arch produces (*n*),
For fingeing fowl, or viler ufes.

---

ther, who liveth at the fign of the Mitre and Punch Bowl, in Martin's-lane, is defcended from faid Martin Luther.

(*n*) *That Journal which the Arch produces*]—The Freeman's Journal is printed at St. Audeon's-Arch, in Old Bridge-ftreet, Dublin, where, contrary to law, there is no printer, nor any other perfon who anfwereth queftions, but an old woman who is dumb. The following anecdote happened once to the printer hereof. A gentleman came to his fhop whom he had put amongft the deaths in his Journal the day before, and was much enraged to find him-felf dead, as it occafioned fome confufion by thofe who were in his debt coming to demand what was due to them, whereupon the author hereof acted in this manner, Sir, faid I, 'tis impoffible for me to tell whether you be alive or dead, but I'm fure I gave you a very good character in my Journal. The gentleman was fo pleafed with the repartee, that he laid out thirteen fhillings and four-pence half penny before he left my former fhop in Eflex-ftreet.

How

How chang'd from him whose noble rage,
Brought great Guftavus to the ftage,
And rous'd the Patriot's God-like fire,
In ftrains which Stanhope might admire !
Now Metjus' fate and his are one,
By all he's torn, that's true to none.

MACRO, with college duft befprent (*),
There mingles to give malice vent,
With various tongues thick fet as Fame,
And ev'ry tongue difpos'd to blame.
In ftudious Macro may be feen,
The copious Polyglot of fpleen :
He fearches old and modern lore,
To learn to hate his neighbour more ;
Fond of men's follies and their vices,
As beggar of his fores and lice is ;
With eyes like fox, and mouth like fhark,
That feems lefs form'd to fpeak than bark:
Let others while their bowls they quaff,
Diftend their lungs with heart-felt laugh;

In

(*) MACRO, *with college duft befprent.*] —We
have not been able to difcover whom the author
intendeth to defcribe in thefe verfes : but fome ingenious friends conjecture that it is fome rev. gentleman, who underftandeth many languages, and
keepeth a play-houfe Mifs.

In fhort fhrill fhrieks of fiend-like glee,
He proves his rifibility.
His knowledge, like a treacherous beacon,
Holds out falfe lights to the miftaken,
And when they wander from their way,
Humanely leads them more aftray.
Yet Macro, whofe peculiar pride
Is to expofe a friend's blind fide,
Can to more glaring foll/ ftoop:
Himfelf a bankrupt *player*'s dupe.
    There bafhful B———n once was feen,
Miftaking dullnefs for the fpleen;
Who fays, unfays, agrees, difputes,
And his own arguments confutes.
How eloquent in fhrugs and fighs!
In uplift hands, and winking eyes!
What fupplication, what contorfions!
His words half form'd, his thoughts abortions!
Such wriggling, grafping, pawing, leering,
You know not if its praife, or fneering.
Such fudden ftops, and circumflections;
Such prefacings, and interjections,
With " Ah, good Heaven!" and " Oh, my
        " God, fir!
" I'm wrong, I own, I kifs the rod, fir;
" There's weight and fenfe in all you utter."
——Mere prologues to an egg and butter;
                                That

That did not pudding sleeves declare him,
Some antic Scaramouch you'd swear him.
Yet underneath that form uncouth,
Dwell learning, piety, and truth;
And no distortion can they find,
Who view him only in his mind.

But oh, what power more dull than sleep,
Does o'er my torpid senses creep?
Does Morpheus shed his poppies round?
Do fresh-pluck'd cowslips strew the ground?
Do harps Æolian lull my ear?
Are drones of Scottish bagpipes near?
Do beetles wind their drowsy horn?
Are gales from swampy Holland born?
In vain with snuff my nose I ply,
In vain the power of salts I try,
I yawn—I nod—for Cl—ke is nigh (*p*).

Let

(*p*) *I yawn—I nod—for Cl—ke is nigh.*]—The
rev. Dr. Cl—ke, Vice-Provost of Trinity College,
Dublin. He hath a very fine taste for poetry,
which plainly appeareth by the specimen annexed
to this piece, as it was first published.

*On a Lady's forgetting her Riding Hat. Written by the
rev. Dr. CL—KE, when Vice-Provost of Trinity
College.*

I.

Fair Anna had no heart to give,
So left her head behind;
Bright MINA on whose smiles I live,
Was not by half so kind.

Let mists and fogs invest my head,
Let all the fathers pen'd be read,
Bid B——nt recite his speech (*q*),
F———ns plead, or Garnet preach (*r*) ;

Set

II.

Both head and heart she with her brought,
    And both she took away,
And with her carried all she caught,
    THAT's all THAT gaz'd THAT day.

III.

Ye nymphs that o'er nine wells preside,
    Instruct the willing fair,
To give their hearts, whate'er betide,
    And hands when they come here.

IV.

So when we see St. John's great eve,
    The fires that round do move,
Shall each instruct us to receive
    A hand and heart that glow with love.

(*q*) *Bid B——nt recite his speech.*]—The earl of
B——t, Knight of the Bath ; famous for his eloquence and personal accomplishments.

(*r*) *F——ns plead, or Garnet preach.*] —Counsellor John F——s.—Doctor Garnet, Bishop of
Clogher. He wrote an excellent Paraphrase on
the Book of Job.—The whole edition may be
found at my shop in Parliament-street.

Set mayor and aldermen before me,
Bid everlaſting C——ll bore me,
'Tell o'er again a thrice-told tale,
Drench me with Port or ropy ale,
Be opium mingled with my drink,
My hands ſhan't fold, nor eye-lids wink;
But theſe vain boaſts avail not now,
More pond'rous Cl——ke to thee I bow.
When wilt thou eaſe the groaning town,
Thou old caſt troop-horſe of the gown?
What haſt thou with the world to do,
Or what the world to ſay to you?
Thou can'ſt not now in amorous glee,
Write madrigals to *fifty-three* (s);

And

(s) *Write madrigals to fifty-three.*] —Various are
the conjectures of the learned on this paſſage. Mr.
Kavanagh is of opinion, that it alludeth unto the
political diſputes which raged in the year fifty-
three; in which the Doctor may be ſuppoſed to
have wrote madrigals, to appeaſe the minds of the
people. My nephew Todd inclineth to believe,
that ſomething is intended which he can't diſcover.
For my own part, I opine, that it only referreth
to the age of the lady, who had attained her fifty-
third year. It certainly is not very genteel to ridicule this paſſion, which is properly called all-
powerful, to ſhew that it ſpareth neither age nor
condition, ſtation nor dignity; not to mention the
example of Anacreon, who was choaked with a
grape-

And frisk in rhymes to please the dame,
Which Christmas bell-man would disclaim;.
Nor can'st thou now in fulsome strain,
Pen Jacobite address again ;

And

---

grape-stone, drinking the health of his mistress
at the age of fourscore: I am myself this instant,
a captive to the charms of a lady who has passed
her grand climacteric, and have addressed many
sonnets to her, in a style no less tender than the
Doctor's, one of which, the most admired by my
friends, I have selected, and venture to publish,
as a proof of my passion, and a specimen of my
poetical endowments.

*To the Widow ——, on her taking a Vomit of Ipe-
cacuanha.*

I.
Soft relict, whose enchanting charms,
   My captive heart enthral ;
Whose frown congeals, whose kindness warms,
   Like honey mix'd with gall.

II.
Say, when the nauseous draught you take,
   On Faulkner will you think ;
And for thy own dear lover's sake,
   His health in vomit drink.

III.
Discharge, bright maid, the foul contents,
   That now your stomach bind ;
But oh ! be sure, at all events ;
   Leave Love and George behind.

And ſcandalizing Alma Mater (*o*),
Of right divine in monarchs chatter;
Nor can'ſt thou, on extortion bent,
Raiſe inſurrections and thy rent (*p*).
Then buzz no more, thou reverend drone,
But to thy kindred earth begone.

IV.

So when in ſieve, well pierc'd with holes,
   Where dregs of fire do reſt,
With ſhaking nought remains but coals,
   To warm the riddler's breaſt.

(*o*) *And ſcandalizing Alma Mater.*]—Mater, as may be found in Littleton's Dictionary, is Latin for Mother. My nephew Todd is of opinion, that the Doctor muſt have had ſome quarrel with his mother: for my own part, how unwilling ſoever I may be to find fault with my author, I cannot but agree with Mr. Kavanagh, and other ingenious friends, that it were better not to divulge family brangles.

(*p*) *Raiſe inſurrections and thy rent.*]—This relateth to a recent fact which paſſed about ten years ago in the North of Ireland. The doctor being unwilling, (for the benefit of the incumbent who was to ſucceed him,) that his living ſhould be let at an under value, inſiſted with his pariſhioners, who offered him twelve hundred yearly, to be paid fourteen; which they thinking unreaſonable went to law, and reduced it to the ſum of 700l. This was the firſt beginning of the inſurrection called the Oak-Boys in the North of Ireland.

What

What figure next confounds my fight,
An Auftrian Count, an Irish Knight (*q*) !

With

(*q*) *An Irish Knight.*]—There are feveral forts
of Knights. Knights of Malta, Knights of the
Garter, the Bath, and Thiftle, Knights of the
Poft, poor Knights of Windfor, Baronets and Bat-
chelors, and the Knight of Kerry. The author
hereof was offered to be knighted in the field, by
the earl of Chefterfield in the Caftle : but confi-
dering that faid honour was to be conferred by the
pofture of kneeling, which is impoffible to the author hereof, by reafon of his member, which he
accordingly refufed to accept, making divers acknowledgments for declining faid honour. This
objection was near being removed by the ingenuity of my worthy friend a Sixth Clerk, who befides his being a great fcholar and critic, is alfo a
moft excellent mechanic, and contrived a leg of
cork, with a fpring joint in the knee, and turning
out its toes as naturally as one made of flefh and
blood, and in this leg I practifed the pofture of
knighthood by genuflexion, my friend holding a
drawn fword over my fhoulder, but being too
quick at the third rehearfal, in attempting to get
up, after faid friend had pronounced the words
" Rife up Sir George," I unfortunately fnapped
the fpring, and fell on my chin to the ground, fo
as to be much bruifed, and would have been fore,
but for the ufe of a falve, which is fold by my nephew Todd, for bruifes, maims, contufions, dif-
locations and other fcratches, in Parliament-ftreet.
When the above leg is repaired, I propofe accept-

D 2   ing

With doleful phiz prefaging wonder,
Much German pride and Irifh blunder (r);
Which patriots, courtiers, ftill expofes,
Miftaking both their wit and nofes (s).

No

---

ing the order in it, which I am told his Excellency
the Lord Vifcount Townfhend is willing to confer
upon me in the fame manner as the earl of Chefterfield.

(r) *Much German pride and Irifh blunder.*]—The
Germans are fuppofed in general to be a proud
people : Julius Cæfar, and Mr Nugent, give them
this chara&ter.   The Irifh are very unjuftly charged for a particular talent in blundering; but it is
well known, that no people exprefs themfelves in
their native tongue, the Englifh, with more perfpicuity and precifion.   The dean of St. Patrick's,
who tho' born and bred in Ireland, always declared
himfelf, when fober, to be an Englifhman.   It
will not, I hope, be confidered as prefumption,
that I add the authority of my Journal, which is
confidered as a ftandard of our language ; whereas
I have always confulted the particular property of
di&ion, and may be bold to challenge any author
now extant, for fuch a variety of tra&ts, written
in fo unblemifhed a purity, without any abbrevia-
tion of terminations, and abounding in the beft
chofen epithets.

(s) *Miftaking both their wit and nofes.*]—This
hereby referreth to the knight's putting the fpeech
of one member of parliament into the mouth of
another by miftake, which was not fair play ; and
likewife

No brain but his cou'd e'er contain
Stories so vapid, old, and vain ;
So Plutarch tells of poison cold,
Which ass's hoof alone can hold.
Humour and mirth no more are found,
For C———ll casts a gloom around.
Lethargic dullness loads each eye,
Ev'n dunces please, when C———ll's by !
Thus, sunshine, sparks from flint conceals,
Which darkness of the night reveals.
In Pliny's learned page it's found (s),
That lightning cannot sea-calves wound (t) ;

Congenial

———

likewise alludeth to the old custom of formerly
reckoning members of parliament in voting, by
their noses ; but as this occasioned divers mis-
takes, when the tellers were not sharp-sighted
enough, and could not see those members that
had small or no noses, and sometimes reckoned
those that had large ones for two, it was therefore abolished, and members are now counted by
their bodies, which is generally larger, and pre-
venteth all confusion.—A particular act of parliament was made in favour of the nose, called, The
Coventry-act, to prevent its being cut off, and
other accidents with impunity.—The famous Mr.
Quin, the comedian, with whom I was likewise
acquainted, advised a friend who was subject to be
pulled by the nose, to soap it, whereby it might
escape and slip through the fingers, this not being
forbid in the Coventry-act.

(s) *In*

Congenial is the dunce's matter,
Callous to wit and pointed satire.
Unfatisfy'd with nonfenfe faid,
He's now refolv'd to read us dead,
With pamphlets naufeating he'll puke us,
On Lord May'r's feafts and Doctor Lucas (*u*).

He

(*s*) *In Pliny's learned page, &c.*]—Pliny wrote many books, and was killed by Mount Vefuvius falling upon his head, though he always wore a pillow faftened to the top of his wig, to fave him from that accident.

(*t*) *That lightning cannot fea-calves wound.*]—An animal that feldom appeareth on our fea-coafts, unlefs to fifhermen in the main ocean.

(*u*) *On Lord May'r's feafts and Doctor Lucas.*—A very remarkable apothecary, and member of parliament. He lived on Ormond-quay, in Dublin, at the fign of Boyle's-Head, who was a famous druggift. He was banifhed from Ireland by a vote of the Houfe of Commons, which confined him to Newgate. He returned to his native country by the fpecial mercy of his Majefty, whom he hath always continued to oppofe (for his good) in two parliaments, where he reprefenteth the city of Dublin. This gentleman unfortunately died between the different editions of this work, which prevented that accident being mentioned at firft. Being one of his conftituents, and having a fcarf at his funeral, riding in my chariot, which I borrowed from one of the fheriffs, when the greateft peers and patriots walked on foot, I thought

it

He fings of·beggars blind and·dark,
Like fome old fnuffling parifh clerk :
For ftanzas vile he racks his brain,
And vainly mimicks Howard's·ftrain !

He

---

it my duty to celebrate his memory by the following paftoral Dirge, which I fent to the Freeman's
Journal, of Saturday Nov. 9th, 1771, which I
knew it would pleafe the Doctor to have it inferted
in his favourite paper, under the title of Corydon.
—The reader will obferve that I have taken notice of the miferable, diftreffed, diftracted fymp-
toms in which the Doctor has left the kingdom
in general, no cocks crowing night or morning,
nor violets or primrofes blowing in our pleafure
gardens, the Doctor having died when King
William was born, it being the fourth of November, 1771.

Sacred to the Memory of Doctor CHARLES LUCAS.

I.

Come every Nymph and every Swain,
Ev'ry·Dryad of the Plain,
Ye Naiads from your Streams emerge
Join me in the mournful Dirge.

II.

Tune your reeds to folemn found,
With cyprefs ftrew the hallow'd ground,
For ah! your faithful Corydon
To the Elyfian field is gone.

See

He writes, he hobbles, bows, and leers,
To gain a feat among the peers ;
And ev'ry abject art he tries,
To prove he's qualify'd to rife.

III.

See the primrofe droops it's head
The violets fade, the daify's dead ;
Each flow'r in forrow dies away,
The kids and lambkins ceafe to play.

IV.

The tuneful race in every grove
Neglect their fong, neglect their love.
The village cock forgets to crow,
And grief fits perch'd on every brow.

V.

Hark the folemn tolling bell,
Rings his laft, his funeral knell :
See the weeping train approach,
The black plum'd hearfe and fable coach.

VI.

Lo Ierne by his fide
Fainting mourns her greateft pride,
Sighing o'er his dear remains,
Her beauteous cheek with forrow ftains :

VII.

Tune your reeds to folemn found,
With myrtle ftrew the hallow'd ground;
For ah ! your faithful Corydon
To the Elyfian fhades is gone.

With

With panegyric he befpatters,
Degrading him he meanly flatters.
Ah! purblind knight! thy arts mifplac'd,
Think better of a Townfhend's tafte :
Fools only will fuch praife affume,
As Hottentots think greafe——perfume.
Mark with what eafe his brain creates
Speeches ne'er *fpoke*, mifcall'd Debates,
'Till at the goddefs Dulnefs' fummons,
He makes one C———ll of the commons (*v*).
Thou, Hutchinfon (*w*), whom every mufe
With winning grace and art endues,
Whofe power 'gainft prejudice contends,
And proves that law and wit are friends,

(*v*) *He makes one C———ll of the commons.*]———
Doubts having arifen how the deficient vowels are
to be filled up, I confulted feveral friends : my
nephew Todd imagineth it meaneth caudle, a
liquor drank by lying-in ladies, as it is compofed
of feveral mixtures : (I think it beft when it is
ftrong of the white-wine.) Mr. Croker very ingenioufly hinteth, he makes one *cartfull* of the
commons; that is, the commons all move together
in the fame machine. I think, with fubmiffion to
better judgments, that the word *dungbill* removeth
all difficulties, and correfponds exactly with the
author's meaning, and with every thing but the
text.

(*w*) Right Hon John Hely Hutchinfon, Prime
Serjeant and Member for the city of Corke.

In

In that promiscuous page alone
By letters J. H. H. art known.
In thee Malone (*x*), the nation's boast,
Precision, law, and sense are lost.
Andrews (*y*), who knows, with various skill,
To rule the passions at his will,
Who like a wise musician seizes
The tone which best his audience pleases,
Wonders to find VIVALDI sunk
To a vile scraper, blind and drunk.
How oft on polish'd Osborne's (*z*) tongue
Pleas'd the attentive Senate hung?
While parties emulously strove
Which most should praise, what all approve.
Now view him in thy faithless strain,
Pert, peevish, and perplexed as M———ne (*a*).

(*x*) Right Hon Anthony Malone, Member for the county of Westmeath.

(*y*) Right Hon. Francis Andrews, Provost of Trinity-college, and Member for Londonderry.

(*z*) Right Hon. Sir William Osborne, Bart, one of the commissioners of the Revenue, and Member for the borough of Dungarvan.

(*a*) Sir William M———e, Bart. lately a Privy-Counsellor, and at present Member for Carysfort. He is supposed to understand hand-writing and accompts as well as any book-keeper in Meath-street; he is very fond of cyphering and arithmetic, and every day wanteth to know more of them.

                                        Gisborne

Giſborne (*b*) who ſays—juſt what he ought,
Who weighs, condenſes every thought,
Whoſe logic, faction can controul,
And ſtrike conviction to the ſoul ;
With energy no longer pleaſes,
But worſe than babbling Cr——m——r teazes (*c*).
Think, falſe retailer, how each ſprite,
Will haunt thy ſlumbers every night,
While theſe dread ſounds invade thine ear,
And chill thy conſcious ſoul with fear.
" Where's Pery's (*d*) deep ironic ſenſe ?
" Where Flood's (*e*) impetuous eloquence ?
" Where witty Harward's (*f*) well-timed jeſt ?
" In thy cold tale ſo ill expreſs'd ?

" Where

(*b*) Major General James Giſborne, Member for
Liſmore.

(*c*) John Cramer, Eſq; Member for the borough
of Belturbet, and ſeventh couſin to the E——l of
L—s—h.

(*d*) Right Hon. Edmond Sexton Pery, Speaker
of the houſe of Commons, and Member for the
City of Limerick.

(*e*) Henry Flood, Eſq. Member for the borough
of Callan.

(*f*) The late Counſellor William Harward,
Member for the borough of Laneſborough, he was
remarkable for wit and humour, and told many
pleaſant ſtories and ſprightly bon mots, viz. ſeeing
once an officer of the Light Infantry who was very

" Where Langrishe (g), French (h), and
　　" Brownlow (i), gone ?
" Where the bright flame of Hamilton (k)?
" Dull Chemift !——all exhal'd and fled !"
——Thy caput mortuum in their ftead.——

　　But whither, Clio, wou'dft thou rove,
Fond they defcriptive pow'r to prove ?

————————————————

little, with a large plume of feathers in his cap,
(faid the counfellor) " If he had but a cork in his
" tail one might make a fhittle-cock of him :" and
at another time meeting a young 'Squire who was
juft returned from abroad, and very conceited,
" He is" (faid the Counfellor) " fomething like
" my grey circuiteering horfe, the worfe for tra-
" velling."　Thefe bon mots my friends tell me,
are not to be compared with fome of my own, viz.
what I faid to the gentleman who was angry at
being killed by my Journal, which will be feen
farther on in thefe annotations; alfo to the Earl of
Chefterfield, on faid Earl's complaining that the
letter and paper of my Journal were not of different colours, with many others too tedious to
infert.

　　(g) Hercules Langrifhe, Efq. Member for the
borough of Knoctopher.

　　(h) Robert French, Efq. Member for the town
of Galway.

　　(i) Right Ron. William Brownlow, Member
for the county of Armagh.

　　(k) Right Hon. William Gerard Hamilton, Efq.
Chancellor of the Exchequer, and Member for
Killybegs, in the late parliament.

4　　　　　　　　　　　　Refume

Refume the theme, refign'd too long,
Let Howard's praife conclude the fong.
Mæcenas puff'd by ev'ry quill (*l*),
Sits higheft on the three-fork'd hill:
And lives for ever by the praife
In Horace's and Virgil's lays (*m*),

                    Yet

(*l*) *Mæcenas puff'd by ev'ry quill.*]—Caius Clinius Mæcenas a great lover of learning, and learned men. For his hiftory, and that of the Emperor Auguftus, and the whole policy of his reign, fee Littleton's Dictionary.

(*m*) *In Horace's and Virgil's lays.*]——They are both to be had, from the hours of eight in the morning till twelve at night, at my fhop in Parliament-ftreet.

I have now gone through the feveral paffages of this admired poem, which I thought required any illuftration or comment, and the reader will judge how far I am qualified for the duty of a commentator; though the fuccefs I have already met with in that capacity, leaveth me little room to doubt of the public indulgence. It would be ungrateful, did I not take this public opportunity of returning my thanks to the many learned friends who have favoured me with their affiftance in this arduous undertaking: they are fuch a catalogue of names as would do honour to the greateft wits of antiquity; and the man who can boaft of the friendfhip of Mr. Dean, fixth-clerk; Mr. Dexter, keeper of the Four-Courts Marfhalfea; Meff. Kavanagh and Croker, attorneys at law; Mr. Thomas Mullock, notary-public, in Skinner-row;

                    and

Yet not one ftanza of his own
Has made the poet's patron known.
While Howard to unborrow'd fame,
By his own works afferts his claim :
Then let a double wreath reward
The mufe's patron and their bard.

---

and alderman Emerfon, of the Spinning-wheel,
Caftle-ftreet ; need not be afhamed of putting his
name to any work, in which they have been his
coadjutors. My nephew, Thomas Todd, has been
fo often mentioned in thefe notes, that 'tis unne-
ceffary to fay any thing in his praife, farther, than
that he is an acute critic, a great traveller, and I
have always found him very faithful and diligent
in his duty, as my foreman.   To him, therefore,
this work is infcribed by

His fincere friend, and paternal uncle,

GEORGE FAULKNER.

NUMBER XLVII.

Tunc omnia venia. SALLUST.

The SALE *of the* PATRIOTS: *A* DIALOGUE. *In imitation of* Lucian's AUCTION *of* PHILOSOPHERS.

Jupiter.

COME, Mr. Mercury, fince there is a change in adminiftration, produce the patriots, and fell them to the higheft bidder: Lord Sancho under-rated them, and did not think them worth his money.

Mercury. I have been laughing at the rogues thefe five years, and expofing all their vicious qualities; the public have *now* fuch a contemptible opinion of them, that there will be few purchafers : however, I'll try. Come; gentlemen, who bids for thefe honeft, worthy, virtuous fenators, defcended from the patriots of *fifty-three*, and of the fame principles?—— The firft I prefent is the moft high, moft mighty, and puiffant D—— of L——. I fet him up at five guineas—Don't mind his looks, he has not feen fun or moon thefe feven years,

(except

(except at Lord Valentia's trial, and then he did not ſtay to give his vote.)——He would bring in more money than the elephant, if he were ſhewn for an Ægyptian mummy. Who bids for the great CRUM-A-BOO, and the head of the F——s?——If any of the corporation of Taylors purchaſe him, they ſhall have the M——s into the bargain.—— I wiſh Lord Sancho would buy him, he might ſave him many a pound, by keeping his accounts. He knows how many grains are contained in a peck of oats, and can diſcover whether the grooms feed the horſes properly, by inſpecting their dung. He is finely qualified to *aſſiſt* Mr. M——ng——n, in dividing a farthing into *centeſſimal* parts, as little Butler has too much wit for his grace. Beſides, he has an excellent hand at drawing up a MEMORIAL!—— I wiſh my printer would buy him;——it is the only chance he has of being paid for his election advertiſements. Come, gentlemen, juſt a going.——Ten guineas only bid for the D—— of L————. Why he is worth more to make a Lord Juſtice of: he has ſerved in that capacity already, and carried a money bill through the council, with as much zeal as old Poynings.——Fifteen guineas bid——once——twice—— three times——Sir, he's yours.

Ju-

Jupiter. The D— of L————, fold to Doctor Solomon of Fleet-ftreet, for fifteen guineas !

Mercury. The next is the famous Kilkenny orator, Mr. Fl—d. Varicus and verfatile are his powers, and great his abilities. He fhall grin at a *pattern* for tobacco, and carry off the prize from all the old women in the country.——He is as bold as a wolf-dog, and would make an excellent conftable or bailiff.——I wifh Sir Richard Johnfton would purchafe him, to frighten the Hearts of Steel—— He would be of more fervice than the Riot-Act——His very looks will do the bufinefs—— I fet him up at 5ol. and a cheap bargain he will be at a thoufand. If I don't fell him here, I will carry him to England, and difpofe of him to Sir John Fielding, or the prefident of the Robinhood Society. If the White-Boys were in full march from Kilkenny, I'd fet him aftride to fwing on a turnpike-gate, and, by expoftulating,——menacing,——reafoning,—— and exhorting,——he would perfuade them to lay down their arms and fubmit. His qualifications and vigilance are extraordinary; and like the great Lord Shaftefbury, he always fleeps with his eyes open. —— Sixty pounds bid for Mr. Fl—d, by Sir Ed—d N—nh—m's aunt.——

aunt.——He is worth a great deal more, as he possesses the virtue of an old Roman. Mr. Fl——d is a man of public spirit and integrity, and will never sell himself to the court for less than a Vice-Treasurer's place. Once, indeed, he was advertised at the Custom-house, to be sold by *inch of candle* ; but that's all over. He has continued a steady patriot ever since, and is likely to remain so.——Seventy pounds bid for Mr. Fl——d ;——*once*——*twice*——*three* times———

Jupiter. Set him down to Mr. Sh——d——n; he will make an excellent usher to his new academy, for the study of oratory.

Mercury. The next is a new proselyte to patriotism. He has just read his recantation from the errors of the court ;——he has not gained much credit by it, as most people esteem him a *kiln-dried* convert.——Who bids for honest, facetious Jack P——ns——by ; the most obliging, civil, well-bred man of his time. He smiled in every man's face, squeezed every man's hand, and made the same promises to every man.——This is the identical Jack, who played *prick in the loop* with so many Lord Lieutenants, and cheated them all ;——but the *Old Soldier* was an over-match for him at last. ——I set him up at half a crown, and will sell him on credit.——Three and four pence bid for

Mr.

Mr. P——nf——by, by Bob. B————ch. It's a pity to part old friends—*Once*—*twice*—Juft a going.

Jupiter. Hold—there is a crown bid, by Mr. A——g——n of the Conftitution Club. Why, Jack may do for a waiter there—He is fit for nothing elfe—I hope he would ufe L——gf——d, T——nf——d, and the reft of Lord Sh——n——n's friends well, and not ferve them with fmall-beer when they call for wine.—Mr. P——nf——by juft a going—half a guinea bid by Lord M——ra, F. R. S.

Mercury. I wifh you joy, my Lord! make him your porter, and your vifitors will be prepared at the gate, to relifh your Lordfhip's *veracity* in the parlour.

Jupiter. Enter, Mr. P. fold to the Earl of M——a, for eleven and four pence halfpenny.

Mercury. The next patriot I produce is, Father J—— F——tz——ns. His converfion, like Father Hurly's, was not deemed fincere; *lack of perferment* is the caufe of both.—If any Catholic nobleman wants a chamber counfel, and a domeftic chaplain, let him purchafe Father John. He can act in both capacities, and *either* appear as a Jefuit, or a Newgate Solicitor. His voice is as melancholy as a paffing-bell, or a muffled drum. He never gave an opinion
without

without a *qualifying* IF, to fave his credit. He has made his fortune by that word. His mild confort *once* cudgelled him for requefting the *titular* bifhop of Corke to chriften his fon, IF F——tz——ns, in order to exprefs his gratitude to the monofyllable.——Come, I fet him up at three pence——Who bids?——I'll fell a bargain of him——

Jupiter. Mr. Mercury, you'll oblige by knocking him down to this lady;——fhe has no money, but offers an *Agnus Dei,* and a pair of beads.——Set him down to the abbefs of —— nunnery.

Mercury. Come, gentlemen, the humorous Knight of Clare, Sir L. O'B——n, who always laughs at his own joke, to fave other people the trouble of finding it out. He has excellent talents for chief-joker at a city feaft, and would be reckoned a wit among the aldermen: I wifh our *patriotic* Lord Mayor had made him fecretary, when he difmiffed Mac Dermot.—— Sir L——s is alfo an expert engineer, and thrives like a frog in a canal of putrified water. ——Whoever purchafes him, fhall have the gold box he got from the corporation of brewers for *finking* the revenue, to *raife* the price of patriots.——If any of the common council buys him, the infcription may be altered,

tered, and the gold box will ferve for Sir Ed——rd, without putting the city to the expence of a new one, which they will be fcarce able to afford, as I hear the Surveyor of Dunleary is determined to curtail *their cuftoms*.—— I fet him up at a fhilling. Who bids more? ——Eighteen pence bid for Sir L——s O'B——n, by one of the late worfhipful aldermen of Skinner's-alley.——*Once——twice——three times.——*

Jupiter. Come, Mr. Mercury, be a little brifk ; Lord Harcourt will land before you finifh the auction, if you go on at this rate.

Mercury. You fee how low patriotifm is fallen in this country ; the fale goes on as heavily as a fubfcription for fermons, or Doctor Lucas's monument. ——Come forward, thou Knight Errant of Kilmainham——you fhall not fkulk under petticoats, as you did in the gallery of the houfe at the Augmentation.——Sir Ed——d is qualified for every thing. He is very candid and fincere, for he made an *affidavit*, to convince the public that he is not a man of honour——a point that was never contefted. To prove himfelf a man of fpirit, Ned firft behaved like a lying knave——and then, to apologize for his behaviour, acted like a poltroon. If any perfon doubts Mercury's arguments, *a priori*, let him enquire of Mr. C——, a

tofte-

posteriori. I mention thefe particulars, from my efteem for Sir Ed——d, as I know *they* will recommend him to the free citizens. Ned is a moft affectionate father, and a man of principles —— for he firft lays out his children's money on a purchafe, *then* forfeits his employment, and turns patriot, becaufe he could not obtain an additional falary. In the mean time, he apologifes for his abfurdity, by faying it was at his aunt's requeft. However, Ned is a *True Blue,* and a friend to liberty.——To fhew his REVOLUTION PRINCIPLES, and attachment to the *Houfe of Hanover,* and in defiance of Jack the Batchelor, he *befouled* St. DOULOGH's well in the groffeft manner, and afterwards gave a memorial to the commiffioners, to be rewarded for ferving the revenue. ——Thefe are the qualifications which entitled Ned to a feat in the next parliament, for the city of Dublin: if Mr. H. does not oppofe him, he will certainly carry the election. I fet him up at three farthings——Who bids more?——Two pence half-penny bid for Sir Ed——d, by honeft Georgy C——ck——ne, the agent. The Knight of the Poft will fwear his *pint* decanters, quarts, and erafe his name from an *accepted* bill, and prove it a *forged one.*

Ju-

Jupiter. Come enter *him* fold to George
C———ne Efq. for two pence three farthings.

Mercury. Suppofe we conclude the fale,
by fetting up the Free Prefs of St. Audeon's,
the Committee, and the Writers to fale.

Jupiter. A proper conclufion, Mr. Mercury;
begin then.

Mercury. Who bids for the Writers, Pub-
lifhers, and venders of Treafon and Scandal,
wholefale and retail——The correctors of all
grievances ; the menders of our morals, and
bad pavement ; rewarders of virtue ; punifhers
of vice ; guardians of the conftitution ; fcourges
of tyrants ; midwives to the Mufes ; gentlemen ufhers, and honourable panders to the
Catos, Ariftidufes, and Bruti of Pimlico and the
Poddle ; the terror of alewives, extortioners,
and ladies fafhionable head-dreffes. They can
defcend from the higheft to the loweft ; from
the Exchequer of a nation, to the bills of an
hedge tavern ; from the revenue, to a mutton
kidney———

Jupiter. Hold ! hold ! Mercury ; we can't
difpofe of the Committee without leave of the
King's-Bench ; Judge R——nf——n may perhaps commit you for a contempt of the court,
unlefs Mr. T——ml——nf——n withdraws his
action : we muft poftpone the fale till that

matter

matter is determined.——But, not to lofe time, we may put up that groupe of fecond-rate patriots that are huddled together in the corner: name them, Mercury, and make a lot of them.

Mercury. Come forward, gentlemen. Here R——w——y, M——x——ll, O——e, F——f——e, C——m——r, B——gh, and the old *College bed-maker*, our city reprefentative,——do——put them up at fomething——What, will nobody bid for them? Here, throw in B——ll——m——nt and M——a. Now, gentlemen, feven and fix pence is not a great matter: if they will ferve for no other purpofe, you may fell them to the merchants, and clap them in the niches round the ftatue of Doctor Lucas, in the New Exchange. Lord B——ll——m——nt's fine perfon fpeaks for itfelf; and as to the other, clap a chain round his neck, and a furred gown on his back, and the graveft of the twenty-four has not a more alderman-like appearance.——Fifteen fhillings—— going——going——no body bids more. Gone for fifteen fhillings, to the Exchange committee.

[*Exunt omnes.*

APPENDIX
TO THE
BATCHELOR.

NUMBER I.

In vain to defarts thy retreat is made;
The mufe attends thee to thy filent fhade:
'Tis hers, the brave man's latelt fteps to trace,
Rejudge his acts, and dignify difgrace.
When Interelt calls off all her fneaking train,
And all th' oblig'd defert, and all the vain;
Thro' Fortune's cloud one truly great we fee,
Nor fear to tell that P———y is he.   Pope.

To the Rt. H——ble J—— P—y, Efq.

SIR,

MORALISTS and fage politicians have expatiated largely on the inftability of court favour: you, fir, have experienced the truth of their obfervations. How ungratefully have you been treated for all your paft fervices !

VOL. II.   E   The

The public are pretty well acquainted with your character; but from my particular esteem and regard for you, I shall divulge some anecdotes that must do you honour, and which, from a laudable modesty, you have industriously concealed.

I am vexed to see you reduced to a private station, and no longer presiding at that board where your abilities shined so conspicuous. As a patriot, it must give me the deepest concern, to see you deprived of that influence, which you so wisely exerted in so many boroughs and counties for the good of your country. How many freeholders have you relieved by generously *pensioning* them on the c——st——ms, and indulged with receiving the profits of their employments, without obliging them to submit to the fatigue of the duty.

Superficial observers, sir, have ascribed your late patriotic conduct to spleen and disappointed ambition. They say, that *pensions*, *titles*, and *reversions*, were the only objects you had in view.——That you were piqued at the residence of a chief governor, as it deprived you of all hopes of becoming one of the illustrious *triumvirate* which long governed this kingdom with so much honour; and that your opposition to the court sprung from the most selfish and sordid motives.

But thefe fpecious objections are eafily confuted. Even allowing that you propofed very
extraordinary terms for your compliance with
adminiftration, I am fure, fir, you only did fo,
that they might be rejected with fcorn, and that
you might have a *reafonable* apology for dif-
playing thofe noble principles of integrity and
difintereftednefs, which always glowed in your
bofom, though you had concealed them fo in-
duftrioufly for many years, that even your moft
intimate friends never once fufpected you had
the leaft idea of them. You acted, fir, like
Brutus in Tarquin's court : he affected folly,
to fecure himfelf from the jealous rage of a tyrant ; and you only affumed the corrupt manners of a courtier, to gain preferment.

· Befides, though you had really intended to
fupport the meafures of adminiftration, if your
terms had been accepted, you ftill fhewed a
high degree of virtue in demanding fuch extravagant ones. You meant to convince the
public how fincerely you loved your country,
by requiring fuch a bribe to betray it ; for certainly a man efteems a thing in proportion to
he price he fets on it.

Your enemies, fir, have accufed you with
want of fpirit; I am furprifed at fuch a calumny. You lately gave a moft convincing

proof

proof of your intrepidity in the Houſe of Commons. You were hardy enough to deny a charge, though the evidence of your own handwriting was againſt you. A leſs zealous friend than I am, might be puzzled to defend you; but I can perceive the rectitude of your intentions, even in your deviating from truth. It was in the glorious cauſe of liberty, ſir, that you for once condeſcended to ſwerve from that nice and delicate ſenſe of honour, which you have conſtantly preſerved. An inviolable attachment to your word, a rare quality in a ſtateſman! was one of thoſe peculiarities for which I always admired you. But I candidly acknowledge, that I eſteem you the more for giving up this ſhining characteriſtic, for the ſervice of your country. In that caſe, ſir, a private vice becomes a public benefit; and it is equally true in politics, as in morals, that the end juſtifies the means.

A perſon of your quick ſenſibility, muſt have ſuffered ſeverely on ſuch a trying occaſion. You then had virtue enough to reſign the character of an honeſt man, to attain the nobler name of a patriot. The greater the ſacrifice, the more your country is indebted to you.

As Speaker of the Houſe of Commons, you have gained univerſal applauſe. You were reſolved folved to ftock that honourable affembly with patriots, and, therefore, in contefted elections, you nobly rejected fome members who had an undoubted majority of votes, and would only admit thofe who promifed to fupport your intereft, and the conftitution of their country, as thofe terms are fynonymous.

Some people are amazed, how you could maintain fuch an influence in the Houfe, with that fmall ftock of natural abilities which they invidioufly allow you. But what they malignantly defign as a reproach, turns out the higheft compliment. If you were endued with fuperior parts and fhining abilities, the phœnomenon would be eafily accounted for. Your merit, fir, is the greater, as you have been able to effect fuch grand things by flender means : a general who conquers with a fmall force, acquires greater glory than if his troops were more confiderable.

Your enemies, fir, alfo accufe you of having deferted your grand ally on the Augmentation Bill ; but they do not confider, that, like Shakefpeare's apothecary, *your will never confented.* You were juftly apprehenfive of lofing your employment, and that is a fufficient apology.

E 3

Give me leave, fir, to lament with you, the
degeneracy of my countrymen? I long ago expected that the whole kingdom would have been
in a flame; that petitions and remonftrances
would have been fent up from all quarters.
What can be the reafon of this fupinenefs? Are
they bafe enough to imagine that you defign to
imitate our memorable patriots of 1753? The
conduct of thefe men has been of the utmoft
prejudice to this kingdom: it has made every
Irifhman a fceptic, they doubt the very exiftence of patriotifm. They cannot be perfuaded
to think their rights and privileges in danger;
becaufe a Money-bill was originated in the
council, as it has been the ufual mode of pro-
ceeding for two or three hundred years.——But
the abfurdity of fuch a conclufion is evident:
For at different periods, the fame thing may
have quite different effects: you, fir, were
convinced of the truth of this maxim. In
1761 you fupported the very meafure which you
have fince difcovered to be fubverfive of the
conftitution. You have obferved fomething
dangerous in that tyrannic fcheme, which you
have not as yet thought proper to difclofe. Probably, fir, you are apprehenfive of throwing the
nation into ferments. You have acted like a
fkilful phyfician, who conceals the danger of
the

the patient's case, left the discovery might ter-
rify him too much.

*It is now time, sir, to mention a circumstance
which must render you extremely popular in this
kingdom. As you foresaw with your usual sagacity,
the necessity and propriety of a land tax, you pru-
dently resolved to insert a clause in every new lease
which passed through your hands, in order to throw
the burthen on the tenant, without diminishing the
landlord's rent roll. One gentleman, indeed, after
his lease was perfected, suspected the legality of such
a clause, and was rash enough to consult two eminent
lawyers on the point. Their opinions chanced to co-
incide, and were entirely in his favour. Tho' you,
sir, were acquainted with their sentiments, you paid
no regard to them, but steadily resolved to pursue
your plan, and accordingly served this refractory tenant with an ejectment. He took defence, and
you then commenced a suit against him ; but as you
were always tender of your reputation, and would
rather lose your right than your popularity, you
stopped all proceedings at the beginning of this session *.*

This,

---

* The candid reader will be convinced of the use and
efficacy of Phocion's address to the right hon. John Pon-
sonby, Esq. (on the subject of an intended land tax) by

E 4   perusing

This was a fine example for the landed gentry; they owe you particular obligations for that

---

perufing the following extract from Mr. Caldwell's letter.

" To ARTHUR BAYLEY, Efq.

" On the death of the late Mr. Langrifhe, Lord Befbo-
" rough did me the honour of appointing me his gene-
" ral agent, and I am now to inform you, his Lordfhip
" is willing to fign any inftrument your council fhall ad-
" vife, to exempt you from all poffible apprehenfions of
" being charged with thofe parliamentary taxes you
" feem fo averfe to, on your paying the rent you now
" owe, which has been for the time paft clearly exone-
" rated and difencumbered therefrom; or if you rather
" chufe to furrender your leafe of part of Garryhill, my
" Lord will accept a furrender thereof, on your paying
" the arrear due.

Your moft obedient humble fervant,
" Dublin, 5th June, 1770.

CHA. CALDWELL.

To the Earl of BESBOROUGH.

MY LORD,

IT gives me peculiar pleafure, to find that your Lordfhip has ordered Mr. Caldwell, your agent, to have a
defeafance made of that very particular claufe in one of
your Lordfhip's leafes, which fubjects the tenant to a future land-tax, inftead of his opulent landlord. Probably,
your Lordfhip never faw Counfellor Wolfe's, and the
Attorney-General's opinions on this point of law, till
they appeared in my fpeculations.

As

that masterly stroke of politics : perhaps you were induced to take this step, by obferving how

---

As the fame *illegal* and *alarming* claufe is inferted in all Mr. Ponfonby's leafes, I hope your Lordfhip's example will have a proper influence on him.——When he was a courtier, my Lord, he might have a fecret intimation from the miniftry, that a land-tax would be introduced here, and therefore acted with prudence by fecuring himfelf at his tenants expence: but now that he is a patriot, he can have no reafon for obftinately adhering to this prudential fyftem.—I fhall be pleafed with having an opportunity of blazoning that gentleman's merit, for he is remarkably modeft, and to avoid public applaufe, fo carefully conceals the great fervices he has rendered his country, that even his moft intimate friends are ftrangely puzzled to give me the leaft information about them.

I am told, that your Lordfhip difapproves of his late patriotic proceedings : however, my Lord, Mr. Ponfonby's is a moft extraordinary character; he gained more friends and dependents by empty promifes, than by conferring effential favours:—I hope your Lordfhip will pardon this digreffion, and I fhall now return to my fubject.

I have a fecret fatisfaction, my Lord, in reflecting on the great ufe my fpeculations have been to your tenant Mr. Bayley. He perceived the dangerous tendency of a claufe foifted into his leafe, with great art and difingenuity, and was determined to act with fpirit and refolution.

" A . . . . . . Man, I n, who w . . . . . . brc . . .
" . . . ."

how the insolence of the yeomanry was increased by the Octennial Bill, and probably you

He stated his case with clearness and precision, and
submitted it to Counsellor Wolfe and Mr. Tisdall ;
encouraged by their favourable opinions, he was determined to have the legality of the clause tried. On being served with an ejectment, he *took defence*, and was
then threatened with the utmost rigour of the law, if
he did not quietly submit. Several of the papers rela-
tive to this affair, fell accidentally into my hands. As
I thought it a matter of some consequence, I was determined to lay the whole transaction minutely before
the public, and took care to inclose your Lordship a
few speculations containing my remarks, and Mr. Bayley's very ingenuous narrative. I own that my vanity
is greatly flattered by Mr. Caldwell's letter. Your conduct my Lord, does you honour, and I can assure you,
that I entertain no despicable idea of your Lordship's
understanding, since you have paid so much deference
to my arguments.

As several of your tenants, my Lord, have a right
to the same indulgence shewn Mr. Bayley, I suppose
your Lordship's directions to your law agent, were general, and equally extended to them. I only mention
this my Lord, lest some malignant persons may impute
your Lordship's behaviour to a sinister motive, if Mr.
Bayley should be particularly distinguished.

     I remain,
       My Lord,
         Your L—p's most obliged,
           And most obedient humble servant,
            JEOFFRY WAGSTAFFE.

            con-

contrived this latter scheme to counteract the pernicious effects of it.

Persevere, sir, in your patriotism, and though you should never more fill such an honourable and lucrative employment, as first Commissioner of the revenue, I know you will be rejoiced to find your place supplied by a person generally esteemed your superior, both in integrity and abilities. You will then resemble that illustrious Greek, who was a candidate to be enrolled in the band of heroes that fell at Thermopylæ, and on being rejected, thanked the Gods " There were so many better men " in Sparta."

I have thus, sir, taken some pains to vindicate your character and conduct, from very illiberal aspersion. I thought it more essentially requisite at this time, as with infinite regret, I find most people too apt to credit those invidious sarcasms.

I always considered you as a most amazing person. You are a facetious companion, without borrowing the least assistance from either wit or humour. You preside with equal dignity in the house, and at the head of a pack of hounds ; and your eloquence is equally adapted for either. The same versatile genius made

E 6   Al-

Alcibiades fo extraordinary a perfonage, It is my boaft to have firft difcovered and pointed out a refemblance between you. Others may have courted you in the funfhine of your power; in your fall I addrefs you:

and am, fir, yours, &c.

Y   PHOCION.

NUMBER II.

Deerant quoque littora ponto.   OVID.

To JEOFFRY WAGSTAFFE, Efq.

S I R,

I Am one of your readers, and conftant purchafers of your paper, not merely for the
fake of fome good ftrokes of humour which
occafionally appear; but becaufe it is the only
political paper which gives us facts and calculations, from whence we can form any juft
conclufion on the ftate of our country, and
the conduct of men. Thefe I often fee confirmed by teftimonies, which are laid before
parliament: by authorities of this nature, the
judgmen

Judgment of every impartial man will be determined. I have frequently reflected with concern, that many large fums which have been granted for public works, have been fquandered away in the moft infamous jobbing that ever difgraced a country.——Of all the enormous fums granted during Mr. P——by's adminiftration, how fmall a part was really for national purpofes?——Let any man of common fenfe examine what are called public works, and he will find they are a reproach to the kingdom. Obferve the fhameful work at Dunleary, where the fole intent of the engineer (if he can be fo called) was to have the work to do over again.——Alfo at Wicklow; how many thoufands have been fpent to turn afide the true courfe of the river, and prevent its fecuring the harbour's mouth; whilft a huge expenfive work is directed in a ftraight line out to fea, in fuch a manner, that no fhip can venture to run into the ports in diftrefs, the only *time that fuch a harbour is ever thought of.* Trace this political jobbing regularly along the coaft—behold the jobb of Dungarvan, which coft 1500 l. where aqueducts are made that can fcarce contain water fufficient to drown a kitten ——Confider the immenfe fums laid out on the contemptible forts of Dungannon, Clike, and Kinfale.

They

They are so many drains to the public revenue, and the purses of the people; for they must affect the latter in the second instance, and will be severely felt, notwithstanding the specious clamour of those false patriots, who loudly expatiate on the poverty of the nation, and other difficulties and objections, to raise their own prices and importance.

Though that celebrated work, called the Mother Line, is really a work of public utility, as it is calculated to open an immediate communication between the metropolis, and the interior parts of the kingdom; yet, how has it been executed? ——Infamously —— the levels of which were taken by Mr. Omer, on horseback; whose accurate eye served instead of an instrument. This was *proved* by him on oath, before a committee of the house.

The line of the Canal, pursued to gratify particular people, instead of obeying the rules of nature, and dictates of science, witness the lock-houses built before the line was cut, on purpose to create offices, and bestow salaries on the worn-out domestics of the chief jobbers.—— These expensive offices have cost the nation 10,332l. 18s. 2d. to maintain the supervisors of *a dry ditch.*

The

The new plan to carry on this work by subscription, conveys an idea of public spirit; and, if faithfully executed, may succeed as well here as in England. Though as a present *douceur*, the subscribers propose to convert 77,101l. 12s. 7¾d. of the national money into private property.

We also find, that our collieries have been worked with the same jobbing spirit; and tho' 65,000l. 17s. 11d. have been lavished on the Tyrone and Ballycastle collieries; and though the D——b——n S——ty have endeavoured to reduce jobbing to a regular system, by particular præmiums on that colliery, yet at this day there are not ten tons of Irish coals in Dublin, nor has there ever been a sufficient quantity to lower the price of English coal.

That infamous jobb of the Black Water (or Mallow navigation) on which 11,000l. was granted, for the purpose of supplying the southern part of the kingdom with coals, now lies in the same unfinished state as the Grand Canal, and is now converted by the gentlemen of the country into cascades and fish-ponds.

But of all the jobbs which have disgraced the kingdom, the bridges erected in the city and county of Kilkenny, are the most infamous. —£8500 was granted by parliament, on the

magni-

magnificent plan, and plaufible eftimates, furniſhed by one of his Majefty's engineers, who,
to make them the more expenfive, propofed
they ſhould be built of cut ſtone. The ſum
was granted to execute his plan ;——yet every
traveller knows, that three out of five of thefe
bridges were erected of rough ſtone, by the
country mafon, and in the cheapeſt manner.——
Confequently 4000 l. at leaſt, remains in the
honourable truſtee's hand for repairs !

Various, indeed, have been the fums granted
to this *favourite* county—no lefs than the fum
of 25,250l. to render the river Nore navigable,
though a Norway yawl could not float on it;
and to erect a country bridge, ornamented with
the Ionic order, to terminate a view from the
houfe of that *virtuofo*, Sir William Fownes:
and even when this bridge was deſtroyed, in
the year 1763, it was rebuilt in the fame taſte,
at the public expence, to gratify Sir William's
fingular taſte in architecture.

Thefe, ſir, are only general hints : in my
next I ſhall be more particular.   The hiſtory
of jobbing ſhall be given, with feveral curious
extracts from Sir Richard Cox's book on the
fubject.

I am, ſir, yours,

November 2, 1771.

An Enemy to Jobs.

NUMBER III.

In every jobb to go a fhare,
Canals to cut, and jails repair;
And turn the fields to public roads,
Commodious to their own abodes.   SWIFT.

To JEOFFRY WAGSTAFFE, Efq.

IN my former letter, Mr. Wagftaffe, I freely
condemned all thofe *political* præmiums,
given under the refpectable title of parliamentary grants, which were folely calculated for
the emolument of particular men, or families,
without the leaft tendency to national improvement.   Such bounties were *indirect* bribes,
given by the ariftocratic powers, to maintain
their *local* interefts ; or to *commute* for the pretended patriots filence on *official* tranfgreffions.
The crown, in the interim, loft the means
of providing for the national defence and fecurity ; and the kingdom was loaded with the
additional expence of *making good* the deficiencies which thofe gratifications had occafioned.
—Our late patriotic fervants of the crown,
were *even* pleafed with the public diftrefs, and
never failed (as I am told) to infift on their
own

own terms for extricating both the government and the country from those difficulties, which were the inevitable confequences of their felfifh fyftem. —If the exorbitant demands of the ariftocracy were not granted, government was mifreprefented to the people :—*Hefitation*, in the ftate contractors, to *clofe the bargain*, was called patriotifm, and the deluded multitude was taught to huzza in their favour.

Every independent man muft look down with indignation on the fallacious profeffions, and mean artifices of fuch a miferable junto : every honeft man, every friend to his country, would prevent fuch impofitions for the future. Yet, on the fame principle, he would judici-oufly, and candidly diftinguifh between felfifh jobbs, and national improvements ;—he would liberally contribute to the fupport of our charter-fchools, and that humane provifion for diftreffed orphans ;—every rational fcheme for the ex-tenfion and improvement of our linen manu-facture, would meet with his hearty concur-rence. To complete the plan for rendering the harbour of Dublin more fafe and commodious, is certainly an object of great importance and public utility. In fhort, agriculture, and every ufeful art, on which the population, in-duftry, and the true intereft of a country depend,

pend, fhould meet with every proper encouragement.——Let the national wealth be judicioufly
beftowed, to cherifh our infant arts and manufactures, and not proftituted to gratify a
pampered faction.——Let us not court the people
by diftreffing the crown ; nor diftrefs the people, by any improper compliance with government.

Let us now examine the different jobbs which
have been carried on in this kingdom, under
the fpecious appearance of *public* works. In
the center of the kingdom ftands that difgraceful monument of L——d L———d's, which was
to have been a magazine of corn. When will
that patriot family refund the 3000l. for which
their honour was pledged to the public.——Let
me recommend this enquiry to that *accurate
accomptant, and great financier,* Sir W——ll——m
M——y——ne.

Turn your eyes northward, and behold the
infamous jobbs on that coaft —— an enormous
fum, granted to *eftablifh* a *fifhery* at Balbriggen,
under the pretence of building a *pier,* in a harbour where a packet-boat cannot enter without
grounding ; whilft the deep and capacious harbour of Skerries has been neglected, notwithftanding repeated application from the merchants of Dublin. The late Lord Sh——n——n,
indeed,

indeed, granted the proprietor a douceur of 2000*l*. but he did not live long enough to reap the fruits of his patron's bounty.

Mr. O'H——ra's fifhery on the Weftern coaft, is only known in the *parliamentary accounts*. If that public fpirited gentleman had caught any whales, I fuppofe we fhould have heard of their dimenfions in the papers. He has enjoyed his præmium for years, and if he has caught nothing, it is furely high time he fhould give over that fport.

Behold the dangerous harbour of Drogheda, left *almaft* in its natural ftate, though a fum of money was expended on it by the celebrated Mr. Omer, who was permitted to fquander 500,000*l*. becaufe he was a *convenient* tool to thofe partriotic difpenfers of national benefits. ——Examine the ufelefs piers of Enver and Bangor, built at the public charge, when the North and South rocks, by remaining without lights, prove fo fatal to the mariner: yet, the inhabitants of Dublin, Belfaft, and Glafgow, have repeatedly petitioned for the *ufual indulgence*. It is well known that the inhabitants of that coaft, pay their rents by the plunder of the many fhips caft on thofe projecting rocks.—— In all thefe fpecious impofitions, the chief engineer had the honour of being a mere *nominal* truftee, truſtee, though the jobbers had the modeſty never to employ him.

Is it not notorious, that private fortunes have been made, and eſtates purchaſed, by parliamentary grants?——witneſs the Ballycaſtle colliery. How ſhall I deſcribe the Lagan navigation?——a ſhip ſailed from Belfaſt to the Weſt-Indies, and returned, before a boat from the ſame port could reach Liſburn, which is only ſeven miles. Yet this canal was reported navigable!

The Shannon, that mighty river, ſo celebrated for its barrier againſt the invaſion of the Mileſians, and the efficacy of its waters on *phyſiogouomy*, would yet be no Iriſh river if it had not a ſhare of the public money! However, twelve miles of this chain of *lakes* and *rapids*, which *otherwiſe* might have ſwallowed up the whole revenue, is now carried on by private ſubſcription. The junction of the Shannon with the Breſnaw, is certainly an object of public utility, but what public benefit can ariſe by carrying on the *cut* from Banagher to Bellhavell, through ſuch a deſart tract (where we can only diſcover the towns of Athlone and Carrick) ſtill remains an inexplicable myſtery, except to thoſe immediately concerned in the jobb.

I hope

I hope what I have faid will be favourably received by the impartial and unprejudiced, though I hear my firft letter has difpleafed thofe gentlemen who ftyle themfelves patriots.—I did not dip my pen in the dirt of the day, nor entertain my readers with perfonal abufe, nor virulent invective; — yet the abettors and compilers of thofe decent papers, the Freeman and Hibernian Journals, who trumpet forth the falfeft defamation, were offended. How could I fuppofe that *public truths* could fo far provoke thofe champions of freedom, Mr. F———d and S——r L——ci——us O'Bry——n, as to draw down their cenfure on the *liberty of the prefs*, and leave that invaluable privilege to the protection of the CHIEF SECRETARY, and AT-TORNEY-GENERAL.

Nov. 5th, 1772.

AN ENEMY TO JOBBS.

NUMBER IV.

To JEOFFRY WAGSTAFFE, Efq.

SIR,

I Am furprifed that none of our patriotic pro-jectors ever adopted Sir William Petty's judicious plan for the improvement of this country.

7

country.—" By comparing," fays he, " the
" extent of the territory with the number of
" people, it appears that Ireland is much un-
" der-peopled ; for as much as there are above
" ten acres of good land to every head in Ire-
" land, whereas in England and France there
" are but four, and in Holland fcarce one.

" That if there be 250,000 fpare hands
" capable of labour, who can earn four or five
" pounds per annum, one with another, it
" follows that the people of Ireland, well
" employed, may earn one million per annum
" more than they do now, which is more
" than the year's rent of the whole country.

" If an houfe with ftone walls and a chim-
" ney, well covered, and half an acre of land
" well ditched about, may be made for four
" or five pounds or thereabouts; then two-
" thirds of the fpare hands of Ireland, can in
" one year's time build and fit up 160,000 fuch
" houfes and gardens, inftead of the like num-
" ber of the wretched cabbins above-mentioned;
" and that in a time when a foreign trade is
" moft dead and obftructed, and when money
" is moft fcarce in the land.

" The other third part of the faid fpare
" hands within the fame year (befides the
" making

" making of bridges, harbours, rivers, high-
" ways, &c. 'more fit for trade) are able to
" plant as many fruit and timber-trees, and
" also quickset hedges, as, being grown up
" would diftinguifh the bounds of lands, beautify
" the country, fhade and fhelter cattle, furnifh
" wood, fuel, timber, and fruit, in a better
" manner than ever was yet known in *Ireland*
" or *England:* and all this in a time when
" trade is dead, and money moft fcarce.

" If the gardens belonging to the cabbins
" abovementioned, be planted with hemp and
" flax, according to the prefent ftatute, there
" would grow 120,000l. worth of the faid com-
" modities ; the manufactures whereof, as alfo
" of the wool and hides now exported, would,
" by the labour of the fpare hands above-
" mentioned, amount to above one million
" per annum more than at prefent."

If Sir William Petty's excellent fcheme had
been purfued, induftry and manufactures would
have made a rapid progrefs in this country, and
the common people would have acquired fome
notion of cleanlinefs and decency :— but the
mere improvement of the kingdom (unconnected with parliamentary jobbs) was inconfiftent
with the popular fyftem of Hibernian politics.
Hence originated the wife projects of opening
a com-

a communication between *diſtant parts*, by means of an inland navigation, and of promoting an internal commerce between places that had no commodities to exchange.——Since the year 1723, 323,088l. os. 5½d. has been paid, *out of the revenues at large*, for making rivers navigable——collieries——dry-docks, &c. The defalcation of his Majeſty's hereditary revenue was the grand object, which was invariably purſued with perſevering induſtry, and uncommon ſucceſs. The national treaſure was ſhared among the truſty repreſentatives of the people. If a member wanted *to build a new houſe*, two or three thouſand pounds were granted to *build a pier for the protection of ſhipping*——Nay, ſo judiciouſly were *all public works* conducted, that carpenters, on the credit of making a waterſpout, have been choſen engineers, and received a practiſing diploma from the N——g-t——n Board. Our diſintereſted patriots derived a double advantage from this mode of jobbing ;——In the firſt inſtance, they divided the *ſpolia opima* of their country among themſelves ; and then enjoyed the inexpreſſible ſatisfaction of obliging government to gratify them with places and penſions, to ſupply the deficiency they themſelves had occaſioned.

It was impoffible, Mr. Wagftaffe, for an English nobleman, unacquainted with the views, connections, and families of this kingdom, to break through this corrupt fyftem of petty politics, which was eftablifhed by *uninterrupted precedent and ufage.* Befides, the *undertakers* folemnly profeffed to every Lord Lieutenant, that it was impoffible to carry on the King's bufinefs, without difpenfing thefe *conftitutional douceurs* to country gentlemen, efpecially reprefentatives of counties, who were apprehenfive of lofing their intereft by accepting a bribe in any other way.

This was the true motive that induced Lord Chatham, and the Englifh miniftry to appoint a *refident* Viceroy. The extenfion of our commerce, and improvement of our conftitution, will long diftinguifh Lord Townfhend's adminiftration. A Lord Lieutenant who muft refide *among us for years,* will be ever ready to promote the true intereft of the kingdom, and conciliate the affection of the people——to reduce our finances to order and regularity——to check the parliamentary mifapplication of the revenue.——And to provide a fufficient fund for the maintenance of the civil and military eftablifhments, and for the reduction of the national debt, are objects which fhould engage

the

the ferious attention of our legiſlature.——Let it be remembered, that no leſs a ſum than 1,574,245l. 5s. 9¼d. has been paid out of *the revenues at large*, in parliamentary præmiums, bounties, &c. I ſhall ſuppoſe that half a million of this enormous ſum has been honeſtly, however improperly, expended.——One million *then*, at leaſt, has been proſtituted to enrich and attach men to our ariſtocratic faction.

I am, ſir, yours, &c.

Y   A MERCHANT.

NUMBER V.

To JEOFFRY WAGSTAFFE, Eſq.

SIR,

"IN a free and virtuous ſtate," ſays Rouſ-
"   ſeau, " there ſhould always exiſt ſuch a
" mutual confidence between the government
" and people, that the rights of each ſhould
" not be preciſely defined. Men of taſte,
" reckoned that picture hard, where the out-
" lines are ſo ſtrong as to be clearly ſeen.
" They admire a piece of painting, where the
F 2   " colours

" colours are delicately blended, and the tints,
" which point out every particular object, are
" softened into each other, by an insensible
" gradation." This idea I think just and
beautiful. The warm debates last Saturday,
on the altered Money-bill, evince the truth of
the philosopher's reasoning. It is the undoubted privilege of the people of Ireland, to
be taxed *only* by their own representatives. We
are *only* free, whilst we enjoy this inestimable
privilege, which should always be preserved
sacred and inviolate. But it is hardly to be
expected, that England will ever suffer her
manufactures to be taxed, or any restrictions
laid on her commerce by an Irish House of
Commons. Whether this was not the obvious
reason of the late alteration, I shall submit to
the candid and unprejudiced reader?

It was agreed by doth parties, that the words
" Cotton Or," were a clerical omission: they
were inserted in the Donaghadee transmiss,
though the two other alterations were the same,
in both bills. In the clause, laying a duty of
one shilling per barrel on all herrings imported,
the words " *except British herrings*," were
added. In the clause, laying a duty of six
pence per yard, on *foreign* diapers and damasks
imported, the words " except from *Great
Britain*,"

Britain," were added. It is probable, that an exception was intended by the Commons, in favour of the Englifh manufactures, by inferting the word *foreign*; but as that word in its *ftrict* and *literal* fenfe, might bear another conftruction, to prevent any ambiguity, pofitive and explicit exception was judged neceffary. Britifh herrings indeed are exempted from the duty of *one* fhilling per barrel ; but how " this would open a channel for " Swedifh and Dutch herrings to be imported " duty free," I fubmit to the fagacious Mr. B—ry B—ry to prove. He might as well affert that " excepting Englifh filks and paper, " from the duties laid on French, would be " attended with the fame princious effects."

The *alterations* that had taken place were certainly *inconfiderable*, and if they had not been approved, they would not have been adopted, in the new Money-bill, which is *verbatim*, the fame with the Donaghadee tranfmifs. A motion was made, to poftpone the hearing of this important queftion, till Monday, to fee if any expedient could be devifed to preferve *inviolate* the rights of the H—fe, and, at the fame time, to prevent the material injuries, which the trade, revenue, and manufactures might fuftain, by the expiration of

the

the additional duties, before a new Money-bill could be paſſed. The expedience of this meaſure was the only point in debate. It was ſaid, " That large quantities of gold and ſilver lace, " foreign ſilks, cottons, &c. might be imported " *duty free*, that by a delay of two days, ſome- " thing might be ſtruck out, to reconcile all " parties, and prevent every inconvenience." After ſome debate, the queſtion was put, and carried againſt adjourning. The previous motion, for rejecting the bill, was carried without a diviſion.

The Prime Serjeant and Mr. Perry diſplayed their uſual abilities on this very intereſting point; Mr. B——e, and Mr. L——e, ſpoke ſo pathetically, that Mr. F. who never wept for himſelf, like Cato wept for his friends. He has ſince declared, that his future oppoſition to government, ſhall be *pro bono publico*, neither directed by ſpleen, diſappointment, or malevolence. On theſe conditions, his old friends, the two little *Ajaces*, have promiſed to creep again behind his ſhield, and to ſhoot their arrows from beneath its ample orb.

Every unprejudiced reader, muſt be convinced that the Engliſh miniſtry, had no intention to injure our trade or manufactures, by thoſe alterations, which appeared ſo exceptionceptionable to the houfe. They have even received their approbation, as *they were adopted by them.* Thefe alterations were folely calculated to preferve the Britifh commerce free from any reftrictions ; and did not in the leaft affect the right of taxation, which every Irifhman would maintain facred and inviolable, at the hazard of his life and fortune.

It is always proper to undeceive the public, and expofe the political craft of thofe difappointed incendiaries, who, on every occafion, are affiduoufly active in throwing the kingdom into a political ferment on the flighteft occafion. They refemble the honeft parfon's wife, who put her head out of the window, and alarmed her neighbours by the cry of " Mur-" der, fire, thieves, robbery !" yet, on examination, this *falfe alarm* was only occafioned by her hufband's having innocently kiffed the fervant maid in her prefence.

Many of my countrymen firmly believe, that our rights and liberties, would have been annihilated, if the altered Money-bill had not been rejected by the Commons laft Saturday. Though in the year 1729, the H——fe paffed an *altered Money-bill*, without fervilely facrificing their privilege by doing fo ; as the right

of

of taxation has ever fince been vefted in the representatives of the people. Two fhort extracts from Boulter's State Letters, will fhew the fenfe of the nation on this fubject. " The " Commons and feveral others without doors, " are in a great heat about the alterations, " made by the council in England, to our " Money-bill. I believe a great many will " be for lofing the bill, rather than agree to " the alterations. They are by all, who know " what they are, allowed to be for the better, " but the point infifted upon is, that no al- " teration whatfoever, fhall be made either in " the Englifh or Irifh Council to a Money- " bill. It is certain, the law here, is againft " thefe warm men, and fo are the precedents : " and it is hoped that the majority of the houfe " will be fenfible of the bad confequences " of rejecting that Bill, which will run the " nation much deeper in debt, and that they " will take care that the Bill paffes." In another letter, dated the 20th of December, 1729, addreffed to the Duke of Newcaftle, he fays, " In mine of the 16th, I gave your " Grace an account of the great ferment we " were in here, about the alterations made in " our little Money-bill, by the Council in " England.

" England. Yesterday came on the debate
" about it in the house of commons, and after
" about four hours debate, it was carried in
" favour of the bill, 124 against 62. There
" have been other divisions since upon every
" step of the bill, with great inequality; but
" the first was the great trial."

To check every extension of prerogative,
and maintain the constitution in its original
form, is the peculiar and indifpenfible duty
of the Commons. A generous and fpirited
oppofition to government, founded on honeft
and difinterefted principles, muft always be
for the benefit of the people—but faction, under the fpecious difguife of patriotifm, produces
national calamity. It may be compared to
the juice of the plant *fpurge*, which will blifter
the fkin, though it refembles milk in colour,
and confiftence.

I am, fir, yours,

December 28th, 1771.

A SENATOR.

Q

NUM.

NUMBER VI.

Quid ? fi quis vultu torvo ferus & pede nudo,
Exiguæque togæ fimulet textoie Catonem;
Virtutemne reprefentet morefque Catonis.

Hor.

To Jeoffry Wagstaffe, Efq. *

SIR,

EVERY political zealot thinks himself
qualified for a legiflator; to maintain the
conftitution in its original form, he efteems
too flight a tafk, and a degradation of his fuperior abilities;——under the fpecious difguife
of patriotifm, he would abrogate thofe falutary
laws, which the wifdom of our anceftors eftablifhed, and *fubftitute* the crude conceptions of his
ill informed and perverted judgment. A modern
patriot acts with the public fpirit of Cæfar,
who robbed the Capitol of gold, and replaced
it with gilt brafs.

In my former letter, fir, I afferted the *conftitutional* right of the Commons in the ftrongeft
and moft explicit terms. I faid, indeed, " It

---

* This was written in Anfwer to a Letter figned Jean
Jacques Rousseau, in the Freeman.

" could

" could hardly be expected that England will
" ever suffer her manufactures to be taxed, or
" any restraint laid on her commerce by an
" Irish House of Commons. That those al-
" terations in the Money-bill, which appeared
" so exceptionable were solely calculated to
" preserve the British commerce free from any
" restrictions, and did not in the least affect
" the *right of taxation*, which every Irishman,
" would maintain *sacred* and *inviolable* at *the*
" *hazard of his life and fortune*." I shewed that
the Commons, in the year 1729, had passed an
altered Money-bill, without abridging their
own privilege, or betraying the rights of the
people, which are effectually secured by the
power of *rejecting*, constitutionally vested in the
House. How are these facts answered by the
personated Rousseau ? He amuses the reader
with an abridgement of Mr. F———d's tedious harangue on the same subject last session,
when that elaborate and ingenious orator de-
claimed three hours and a half, without speak-
two minutes to the question. He took infinite pains to shew what the constitution of
Ireland was, before the reign of Henry VII.
After an ostentatious display of great political
knowledge and logic, in proving a point that

F 6

was

was never contefted, he drew this very extraordinary conclufion from his premifes : " That
" the conftitufion of England and Ireland were
" ftill the fame ;" ——though the latter was
altered and new modelled by Poynings' law,
which introduced and perpetually eftablifhed
an effential difference between the political
conftitutions of both kingdoms !——The late
alterations in the Money-bill were adopted by
the commons. We have therefore the fanction and approbation of the Houfe for *their*
propriety.

Let me now, fir, anfwer your perfonal addrefs. You fhew little of that liberality of
fentiment, (which you recommend) by invidioufly pointing out military men, as enemies
to freedom, by profeffion. In the field, they
are ever ready to defend the rights of their
country.——In the clofet, they remember, that
a Britifh foldier owes his fovereign the legal
obedience of a freeman, not the implicit fubmiffion of a flave. On this generous principle
they acted at the Revolution. " JAMES," fays
Lord Bolingbrook, " Drew out his army——
" but it was a Britifh one."

In the fame ftrain, you excruciate the unfortunate and aged Roufleau, by fubfcribing his
name

name to " Clandeſtine Calumny." That original and ſentimental philoſopher, the friend of liberty and truth, you degrade into a caluminator, and an advocate for faction. Your conjectures and your arguments, are equally groundleſs. The * perſon falſely, and *maliciouſly* ſlandered, was not the writer of that Batchelor, which provoked your reſentment, nor was it a joint labour. Preciſion and eloquence in argument, graced by the traits of a brilliant fancy, acquire new luſtre by a claſſical correctneſs and poliſh which diſcriminate his ſtyle : his pieces appear like good prints finely *illuminated*. I ſhould be jealous of his aid, for, like Vortigern, who called in Hengiſt, I might be ruined by my ally.

You kindly conſign " Military men to the " dance and theatre for amuſement." Suppoſe we ſhould deviate beyond the bounds you preſcribe, and frequent the Senate. Suppoſe we ſhould *dare* to laugh at a pompous declaimer, who ſeems to have ſtudied geography in the farce of the Upholſterer, inſtead of Salmon's Grammar. He who firſt pointed out a method by which " our natural enemies might " ſtrike at the very *vitals of our conſtitution*, by

* C—pt—n J—ph—n.

" embark-

" embarking at Calais and landing at Dover !"
He who proved how impracticable it was for
the French to land in the *Southern* or *Western*
parts of this kingdom, by afferting " That
" they muft fail up the Englifh channel, and
" force their way through the Britifh fleet !"
Who fhewed *equal* fkill in hiftory, by telling
the Houfe, that " When one of the mob fpit
" in Timoleon's face and buffeted him, the
" generous Greek inftead of refenting it, re-
" turned the gods thanks, that liberty was
" firmly eftablifhed in Syracufe !" Suppofe we
fhould paint the man, who repays *perfonal*
friendfhip by perfonal abufe. Who points his
invectives in the fenate, againft thofe who
plead his caufe without fee in the courts.
The man whofe bombaft and diftorted figures
(to ufe his own expreffion) " might make
" the very benches vocal."

When faction and patriotifm are fynonymous
terms—when a B—wn—w and a P———y,
in the year 1753, deigned to vote for an
altered Money-bill, though now they *affect* to
believe it *unconftitutional*—— when we obferve
fuch glaring inconfiftencies and contradictions,
it is proper to undeceive the public and expofe
the craft of political incendiaries. I have a

right

right to scrutinize with severity, the *public* characters of men, when truth and justice are my guides: their private actions should be left to the jurisdiction of conscience. I see the Protestant manufacturers drove from their country, by the oppression and extortion of their unfeeling landlords—I see the essential interests of the kingdom neglected, and every means used to promote a breach between this country and England, in order to throw an odium on the administration of Lord T————d: A selfish contest for power, is veiled under an affectation of public spirit. To see a deluded people caressing men who only merit contempt, might even create a suspicion, that a scarcity of good and honest men in the nation, could be the only inducement; as Cato, on observing some strangers at Rome, carrying dogs and monkeys in their bosoms, asked if the women in their country did not bear any children?

I am, sir, yours,

January 7th, 1772.

A SENATOR.

Q

NUM.

NUMBER VII. *

RESPECT for the genius of Rousseau, and veneration for his character, first led me to seek his acquaintance, and to cultivate his friendship : we met like men whose souls had something congenial, and a name in the republic of letters abridged the forms of introduction, and served as a link to that kind of intercourse which subsists between men, unincumbered by the clogs of the world, and the slavish shackles of interest and selfishness. We had called ourselves Philosophers, and as such we were received by those, who did not give themselves the trouble 'of examining into the right by which we became our own sponsors. In return for this complaisance, I thought myself bound to conform to the world, where it did not interfere with my happiness, or require a sacrifice of my principles ; and when I failed to reform abuses, or to rectify errors, I sat down contented with the endeavour, and wished more skill, and better success to my fellow

* This was written in the character of David Hume, in answer to a letter signed Jean Jacques Rousseau, which appeared in the Freeman.

labourers

labourers in the fame undertaking. The citi-
zen of Geneva I foon found was of a very different complexion : an ardent thirft for pre-
eminence in fcience ; a prurient vanity, dif-
guifed under the affectation of much fimplicity
and plainnefs ; an underftanding too fubtle to
be convinced ; and a temper too irritable to be
at peace, made him jealous, difcontented, and
uncomfortable.   The intimacy which enfued
between us, left me no, room to doubt that he
fhunned fociety, not fo much to indulge con-
templation, as to efcape a fcrutiny, which would
reduce him to the level of that herd from which
he had retired.   Heteroclite opinions, and the
fingularity of fectaries, were fure of his countenance ; his was a perfecution of eftablifhments; and to fhake the foundation of fyftems,
confirmed by compact and prefcription, was
his principle purfuit, his favourite pleafure, and
his ultimate ambition.   A retrofpect to the
caufe of his alienation from me, (which became afterwards a fubject for the tables, and
the news-papers of London,) gives me no un-
eafinefs.   Though his mifanthropy rudely
turned back the ftream of my benevolence on
the fource from whence it firft proceeded, yet
it has ftill enough of vigour remaining to flow
towards him in the fame gentle and temperate
                                                    current ;

current; and if he will not use its waters to wash away the stains of prejudice, let them serve as a mirror, where he may contemplate the incongruity of philosophy with faction; and of professions of good will to mankind in general, with rancorous invectives against innocent, and respectful individuals.

" The history," he says, " of the English " nation, first induced him to seek a refuge " among the sons of freedom, as he thought " them; and my *misrepresentations* contributed " to the *captivating error.*"——That is, I have in my history represented the people of England as a free people——my pages contain all the information I could collect on that important subject, and my ideas of the British constitution arise, from the sum of that information. So far then, as I have endeavoured to explain to my countrymen their right to liberty, I am certainly a friend to freedom. " Yet Hume," he says, " is the missionary of corruption, and " applauds the political ethics which himself " inspired,"——The very reverse of his premises will lead to his conclusion. Had he gathered from my writings that Britain had no just claim to freedom, that every circumscription of monarchy was an innovation, every extension of the subject's privileges an encroachment
ment

ment on the royal prerogative, well might this
friend to the natural rights of mankind, have
called the arbitrary hiftorian a miffionary of corruption. What does the mifanthrope mean ?
Is it that my converfation and example are pernicious, and have a more extenfive influence
than my literary labours ? The fuppofition is
abfurd ; and yet without this abfurdity, I know
not how to collect a proposition from his inconfiftent rhapfody.

Let me now confider his argument on a fubject fo often difcuffed in the parliament of Ireland, and in the fugitive publications of that
country. It is immediately palpable from what
political MENTOR, the PHILOSOPHER OF THE
ALPS has imbibed his doctrines of the Irifh
conftitution. The fentiments in his letter are
an abftract of that *fenator's* tenets, whofe capacity and perfeverance have raifed him far above
his competitors in the ftrife of oppofition. That
orator has often perplexed the wife, and afto-
nifhed the ignorant, with fine-fpun fophiftries
on this his favourite topic ; and it is not the
meaneft of his triumphs, that his rhetoric has
roufed the harraffed Rouffeau again to buckle
on his armour, and enter the lifts of contro-
verfy in the caufe of error. It fhall be my endeavour to fhew him he is deluded by a phantom ;

tom; and it will be his duty to thank me for the difcovery.

In reafoning on all conftitutional queftions, we ought to confider what the conftitution and the laws *are*; not what we *wifh* them to be, or what we *think* they *ought* to be; otherwife, we fubftitute fpeculation for reality, and the reveries of every vifionary reformer, for the fubftantial acts which hold nations in obedience to legiflative authority, fince by that coerfion the great end of all civil inftitutions is promoted, and the frame of government preferved in harmony and good order.

He afferts that the commons of Ireland *only*, have a right to propound and model bills of fupply; that the crown of England has *only a negative* on fuch bills, and that it has *no power* to *alter* them. As a friend to the immunities of a generous and loyal people, I am forry to inform him that many laws muft be abrogated, and many precedents fwept from our remembrance, before any one of his affertions will bear the teft of an examination. Let him look to the ftatute of Poynings, by which it is provided, that no parliament fhall be fummoned in Ireland, till the *articles* of the acts propofed to be paffed therein, are firft certified by the governor and council, under the great feal of Ireland.

land In this there is no exception of Money-
bills.——Let him turn to the fourth of Philip
and Mary, which, to prevent the inconvenience
of frequent diffolutions, (and for that purpofe
chiefly) provides, that bills in the ufual form
may be certified to England, during the feffions
of parliament. In this there is no exception
of Money-bills.——Let him confider the Money-
bills which have been brought from the governor and council into the houfe of commons,
and there paffed——Let him furvey the Money-
bills which have been altered in England, and
paffed with fuch alterations by the parliament
of Ireland.——When he has done this let him
recommend to the friends of independence, not
to deny the exiftence of fuch laws and precedents; but, if poffible, to annihilate them :
nor to charge a temperate, and public-fpirited
adminiftration, with attempts to violate the conftitution, when they themfelves are in fact, the
only innovators. He afks, " What fupport
" or exiftence has the ineftimable privilege of
" the commons, that of being their own tax-
" mafters, if a rival and deftructive power be
" vefted in the crown of Great-Britain ?" I
anfwer, that the crown does not exercife the
power, nor pretend to the power of taxing
you ; that your bills of fupply do not become
laws

'laws till the commons have approved and paffed them : and that the modelling (as he calls it) an Irifh Money-bill in England, is no more than propofing to your confideration, for an uncompelled acceptance, one mode of taxing commodities imported into your kingdom, which England thinks preferable to that you have of-fered for her approbation.

So far I have examined and expofed his in-juftice and ingratitude to Mr. Hume, and his ignorance or perverfion of the conftitution of Ireland. It is now time to try, whether he is more candid or better informed in his fenti-ments of the two military gentlemen, who, he infinuates, " are hired to the tafk of wound-" ing with their pens, that conftitution they " are paid for defending with their fwords." A late publication in the Batchelor which he fuppofes to be a joint-labour, (though I am well informed of the contrary) is, he thinks, a fuf-ficient juftification for his contemptuous admo-nition to both the writers, and for his malici-ous accufation againft one of them. I have carefully perufed that paper, and am bold to affirm, that fo far as it goes in regard to the late Money-bill, the pofitions are fair, fenfible, and conftitutional. For the fake of letters, I muft hope, that the author, (let his profeffion

be

be what it may) will often employ his leifure
and his talents on fubjects which he feems fo
well qualified to handle ; let him not abufe the
gifts of nature, and the advantages of educa-
tion, by mixing in fcenes of idlenefs, diffipa-
tion, and vanity : though his ftudies fhould
prove offenfive to the pretended champions of
liberty, and though the philofophic Rouffeau
fteps into the loofe robe of Petronius, and re-
commends, inftead of them, the exercifes of
the dance, and the allurements of the theatre.
His malice is of a deeper dye, when he addreffes
himfelf to the other gentleman ; yet though
there be much venom, there is little vigour in
the fhaft he has aimed at him. Bafely and unjuftly to revile the man to whofe family he be-
longs, and to whofe favour he is obliged, would
be abfurd and immoral. I know from good
authority, the charge is utterly falfe and groundlefs. Suppofing it had even the colour of truth ;
how can Rouffeau be juftified for making it public ? It ftrikes at the fortune, not at the arguments of his imaginary antagonift. If this
kin to *Hermes* entertains an ill opinion of his
patron, that opinion muft have been communi-
cated in the freedom of intimacy, and under
the fecurity of confidence. It muft have been
uttered to the *friend*, not to the *publifher*. He

7   knows

knows no friend vile enough to *betray* such a *secret*; he knows no gentleman wicked enough to *invent* such a *calumny*. As his duty prompted, and his capacity enabled him, he has more than once vindicated the honour of his patron, from the shameless defamations of a licentious press; nor can that noble person one moment admit the testimony of a libeller against the integrity of his advocate, without giving weight at the time, to the same sort of spurious evidence, against his own insulted virtues. The Chief Governor knows why the names of these gentlemen are become the sport of every news paper, and the prey of every anonymous mungrel. It may raise, but it cannot hurt them in his estimation. It is, because they do not look on, and tamely see his name reviled, his conduct misrepresented, and his government rendered odious. It is because they can distinguish between *pretence* and *principle*. It is because they have sometimes wrested the dagger from the hand of the lurking assassin, and turned the point against the magnifico who suborned him. It is in short, because, they have done that in the cause of justice, public virtue, and private friendship, " *quod quisque suos in tali re* " *facere voluiffet.*"

.January 9th, 1772.   DAVID HUME.

Z

NUMBER VIII.

Extremum autem præceptum in beneficiis, operaque
danda eft, ne quid contra æquitatem contendas, ne
quid per injuriam. Fundamentum enim perpetuæ,
commendationis, et famæ eft-juftitia, fine qua nihil
poteft effe laudabile.

CICERO de Officiis.

To JEOFFRY WAGSTAFFE, Efq.

SIR,

PLINY defcribes a fpecies of men with
heads like dogs, who barked inftead of
fpeaking; I fancy our complaining patriots are
lineally defcended from thofe monfters. The
dull declaimers in the Freeman, without either
precifion in their arguments, truth in their affertions, or any knowledge of the fubject they
write on, ftill continue to pour out illiberal invectives on our Chief Governor; though a
moment's reflection might convince them, that
the prefent deficiency in the revenue principally
originated from the management of that able
financier, and incorrupt patriot, Mr. P.

The late Sir Richard Cox conftantly afferted, and proved by the moft accurate calculation, that Mr. P——nf——by's election to the

chair, and supporting him in it, cost the nation one million sterling.   Sir Richard formed his estimate by the several parliamentary grants for different jobbs, including the pensions bestowed by government on Mr. P——ns——by's friends, from the year 1754, when Lord B——s——b——gh was appointed *Lord Justice*, to the year 1764, when Mr. P. vainly imagined himself firmly established by the *family compact.*——In the year 1765, he became chief contractor for doing what was called the King's business, that is, *procuring the usual supplies essentially requisite to the support and defence of the kingdom.*   For thus graciously condescending to serve his country, he enjoyed the invaluable privilege of conducting every jobb in the House of Commons, and of lavishing the public revenue, to influence and carry on elections in the country. Such were the grand objects of Mr. P——ns—— by's administration, when he presided in the house, and at the board.

The expence of the revenue establishment annually increased, from 69,658l. 15s. 2¼d. till in the year 1769 it amounted to 117,714l. 4s. 2¼d.   By this means Mr. P. became intoxicated with power, and fought government, (as BROGHILL expresses it) " in its own ar-
" mour, and with its own weapons, at the
" head

" head of his revenue-legion of collectors,
" furveyors, tide-waiters, fearchers, packers,
" guagers."

If we examine his minifterial conduct, we
fhall find, that inftead of providing for the exi-
gencies of government, by judicious and equit-
able taxes, he loaded the nation with a debt
of 581,964l. 3s. 9¼d. either through inattention or defign ; and fuffered the very laws, on
which the collection of the revenue immediately depended, to be explained away by the fubtle diftinction of lawyers, and the quirks of
fmugglers, agents, and folicitors.——To Mr. P.
We are obliged for the act of parliament to
explain part of the 14th and 15th of Charles
II. by which the revenue has been diminifhed
86,151l. yearly.——Not content with this,
more jobbs were accomplifhed by his unbounded
power in the Houfe of Commons to complete
the defalcation.

When the Lord Lieutenant's firmnefs had
rendered the leaders of faction contemptible,
and baffled every effort either to cajole or intimidate him ; when Mr. P. found himfelf difappointed in all his mercenary fchemes, he at
laft refigned the chair.   Like an afs ftung by
a hornet, he had fmarted by the counfels of the

G 2   Kil-

Kilkenny orator, and was glad to escape from him.

Government, now freed from a disgraceful subjection to state contractors, is in the condition of a person, who on coming to age, discovers the frauds of a knavish guardian : this will appear evident by the following state of the revenue.

	l.	s.	d.
Deficiency occasioned by the explanatory act of the 5th of George III.	86,151	0	4
By six pence per gallon, drawback on rum landed in England—a bounty equally prejudicial to both kingdoms, as it encourages smuggling on their coasts,	64,613	7	0
By an alteration in the excise gallon,	20,000	0	0
£	170,764	7	4

In Aug. 1744, Mr. P. was appointed commissioner : in that year, which ended at Lady-day 1745, the revenue establishment amounted to

l.	s.	d.
54,092	2	2¼

l.   s.   d.

54,092 2 2½

Which in the year ending Lady - day 1759, was   }   83,259 14 1½

—————

l.   s.   d.

Increaſed charge ——   29,167 11 11

INCIDENTS.

l.   s.   d.

Year ending Lady day 1744. } 15,566 13 0

Year ending Lady day 1769. } 31,454 10 1¼

—————

Increaſed charge in incidents 15,887 17 1¼

£ 45,055 9 0¼

Mr. P. thus appropriated the ſum of 45,055 l. for the maintenance of his *civil liſt*. The of-ficers of the revenue, inſtead of minding their duty, employed themſelves in election-jobbing, as the moſt effectual recommendation to their patron.—A total relaxation of diſcipline took place among Mr. P.'s troops. —— Collectors, might embezzle his Majeſty's caſh, and even ſend up falſe returns for their receipts, to apo-logize for not anſwering an acquittance.—If

they

they could influence a *burgess*, or command two or three votes, they were esteemed excellent officers, and received the thanks of the first Commissioner.

Nothing can be more absurd than to see a set of men affecting to be patriots by exclaiming against every thing that tends to improve the revenue. They must know that they ultimately distress their country by this conduct; the civil and military list must be kept up for the sake of the whole; and some gratifications are necessary, not only as rewards to merit, but to alleviate the misfortunes of families fallen from their rank and affluence, who would otherwise be reduced to obscurity and indigence.

The greatest insult, and indeed imposition, on the public, is, to see those who already enjoy preferment, and those who expect it, distressing their country by an affectation of virtue—tho' they brandish the sword of opposition with one hand, the supplicating palm of the other is extended; like the *spiritual* eye of a Swadling preacher, up-lifted to Heaven in a fervour of devotion, whilst the *carnal* one is cast down, to count the shillings, and compute the *godly gains* extorted from a deluded audience.

Whoever

Whoever examines the penfion lift, will find that no families have loaded their country fo unmercifully as our prefent bawling patriots. They even obtained penfionary favours for *years*, that the prejudice they had done their country might not ceafe with their lives, and that they might fhew their ingratitude to government without injuring themfelves.

The public, caught with the mere found of their prefent profeffions, do not fee that the national revenues have been mortgaged, and are likely to be again mortgaged, to fupply the infatiable demand of thofe pampered patriots on a fecond converfion.   This we may expect, whenever their own noife, and the public credulity, fhall raife them to fufficient confequence.

June 25th, 1771.   VECTIGAL.

Q

NUMBER IX.

BROGHILL's ANSWER
TO
SINDERCOMBE.

YOUR letter gave me fome fatisfaction—— not that I admit the authenticity of your

G 4   facts,

facts, or admire the force of your arguments, not that I think the public will be better enabled to judge of the meafures of government, by the communication of your fentiments, or that the Lord Lieutenant will be reformed by the feverity of your animadverfions :—but, as a well-wifher to the perfon and adminiftration of his excellency, I am pleafed to find that a writer of no defpicable talents, is obliged to refort for the materials of invective, to the ftale refufe of news-paper anecdotes, and the exploded calumnies of vulgar detraction. You have collected the remnants of both, with a malicious induftry, and tricked them out in all the tinfel of antithefis, and the fecond-hand frippery of imitated periods. You have kept a reverend eye upon that great Homer of defamation, Junius; and, like your mafter have created a monfter of your own imagination, in order to fhew how ingenioufly you can rail at it.

There is fomething very inconfiftent in the advice with which you begin your letter, that Lord Townfhend fhould think it *worth his while* (your own elegant expreffion) to deliver down unimpaired to pofterity, a name diftinguifhed by the virtue of his anceftors, when, at the fame time, you do every thing to prevent the bene-

fit

fit of your own admonition, at once throwing dirt upon his reputation, and warning him
to take care it may not be fullied.

A writer whofe principal aim, like yours,
is to rail, muft trace up every political event
to a corrupted fource. Accordingly in rejecting fome pretended caufes of L—d T——d's
appointment, your very candour is no lefs malicious than your fagacity, in fixing upon
that which appears to you to be the true one.
The intereft of families is generally the fame,
and a great ftation, obtained by the juft reputation of brothers, is feldom held upon ig-
nominious conditions, or ufed for unworthy
purpofes.

Full of the beft intentions towards the country he was to govern, he opened his firft feffion with the promife of a law to fecure the independence of judges; and why that promife
was not fulfilled in its utmoft extent, muft be
afked, not on this fide of the water, but perhaps of a quondam minifter, whofe jefuitical
politics feldom had any higher view than to
fecure his own department from encroachments,
by impeding the bufinefs and diminifhing the
credit of every other.——The public, however,
have little to regret, as no inconveniencies have
been known to refult from this difappointment,

and the attainment of ten fuch laws, to fecure
what was never invaded, could not be confidered as equivalent to that which was never expected, though fo often demanded, the limitation of parliaments.

It is difficult to determine upon what authority you fo confidently aſſert, that his E——y
never intended, that is, never wifhed to give
either. Is it the fhrewdneſs of your own conjecture ? or has it been fuggefted to you by
that gentleman of *popular manners,* whom you
reprefent fo honourably contending againſt government, in its own armour, and with its
own weapons, at the head of his revenue-legion
of collectors, furveyors, waiters, fearchers,
packers, and guagers ! He, indeed, might have
told you, that, as to himfelf, he never wifhed
fuccefs to the limitation bill, notwithftanding
his pretended zeal for it; that he had found
more than one Chief Governor, on whofe
fympathy he could repofe the infincerity of his
bofom, and knowing little more than the ſtation of Lord Townfhend, concluded that would
operate as it had done before, for the gratifi-
cation of his private views, which were generally inconfiftent with his public declarations.
Were thefe authorities however more powerful,
the ftubborn fact would not bend before them.
We have the law, and the people have paid the
honeft

honeft tribute of their gratitude to him, who
difdained an under-hand ftipulation to obftruct
it, whofe name will appear with unrivalled luftre
in the records of parliament, and whofe memory will be revered while there is any fenfe of
independence, or any abhorrence of oppreffion,
in the yeomanry of Ireland. You next tell
us, that the fuccefs of the augmentation was
the principal object of the adminiftration; and
you impute the mifcarriage to his want of management, though you enumerate a catalogue
of difficulties, which made fuccefs almoft impoffible. Thus hurried along by a rage to cri-
minate, you either confound the charge with
the juftification, or (which is more likely)
you fuppofe the incautious reader may do it for
you.

Some circumftances unfavourable to the
meafure he could not forefee, and others, from
a regard to his own dignity, he could not wifh
to prevent. Of the firft fort were, the clof-
ing the committee of fupply, (which could
not be kept open till the enabling act, pre-
vioufly neceffary for the augmentation of the
forces, was paffed by the legiflature of England)
and the clamours raifed againft the army there,
and in America, for interpofing at the defire
of the magiftracy in both countries, to fup-

G 6   prefs

prefs riots, and reflore order, for which no civil authority was found fufficient. Of the fecond, was the claufe of diffolution in the limitation bill, agreeable to the true fpirit of the
law, as fuch the object of the people's wifh,
and therefore entitled to the recommendation
of government.——But the great difficulty, and
the great offence of all, remains to be accounted
for, the alienation of parties from government.
The public have long known this was the real
caufe of oppofition, but till you appeared, no
one was found hardy enough to impute it as the
crime of adminiftration.   To fee the bufinefs
of the nation conducted without the venal concurrence of a rapacious confederacy, had long
been the wifh and the defpair of the people.
Thofe who reverenced the dignity of the crown,
were forry to fee it degraded by the fupinenefs
or timidity of its reprefentatives.   Too many
adminiftrations had been diftinguifhed by events
of no greater importance than new acceffions
of influence to connections already over-grown,
and the fhameful barter of the favours of government, to fecure the repofe, or to gratify
the avarice of the governor.   No wonder then,
when a new fpirit of activity and difintereftednefs appeared at the Caftle, that new maxims
fhould be adopted, and new pretences held out

by

by the difappointed brokers in parliamentary
traffic —— without changing their principles,.
they fuddenly changed their conduct, and
united all their ftrength to harrafs him whom
they could neither feduce nor intimidate. The
well difciplined cohorts of L——n——r and
S——h——n, fell into the ranks at the firft tap of
the drum ; and the motley bands of P————y
were cajoled and menaced into obedience. A
body of independent irregulars joined the
ftandard, not the caufe of oppofition, and
after difputing every inch of the ground,
victory was decided in their favour by an inconfiderable fuperiority. It required no fmall
degree of fpirit to look this formidable alliance
in the face, and nothing but the greateft cir-
cumfpection could have prevented its being,
ftronger.

So far your capital objection to him as a
ftatefman, is without foundation; yet admit-
ting, as I do, that the fuccefs of the augmentation was his principal object, I fhould be
at a lofs how to defend his fufficiency, had he
again been baffled ; but, to the confufion of
your own argument, you are obliged to acknowledge, that in this meafure he has fucceeded ; and let the voice of truth tell you
how ;——with fuch peculiar felicity, as to give

at

at once new vigour to the crown, and new
fecurity to the people ; to unite in its fupport
the real patriot by his principle, and the
falfe one by his pretence, to leave even jea-
loufy without a fear, and ingenuity without
one colourable objection. But is feems you
are as much offended with the new modification
of the meafure, and the terms upon which it
was obtained in the fecond feffion, as at its
not being obtained at all in the former. You
are hurt to fee majefty defcending from the
throne, and capitulating with the people. I
have never underftood that an amicable agree-
ment between the king and the fubject, for the
mutual benefit of both, has been ever confidered as a degradation of royalty.——The
crown has often made exchanges of a fimilar
nature, furrendering prerogative for revenue ;
and fome of the greateft improvements of the
conftitution have arifen from fuch a commerce.
Had his majefty, or his reprefentative, meanly
ftipulated with *individuals* for the fupport of
his meafures, and, according to what feems
to be the great myftery of your politics, promifed or bribed them into compliance, the
King might then indeed be faid to have defcended from his throne and to have proftituted
the royal dignity.——Your profecution againft
him

him as a ftatefman being clofed, you proceed to arraign him as a fenator and a foldier. An impartial account of his conduct in both thefe relations, would be his beft panegyric and your fulleft refutation. His ample fortune and fplendid expectations, his voluntary en-gagement in an unlucrative and perillous pro-feffion ; the fpirit with which he relinquifhed, and with which he refumed it ; the teftimony of the generals he ferved under, and of the armies he commanded, have all contributed to fet a feal upon his character, and are fuch memorials to his honour, as the moft ingenious malice will never be able to efface.

You are grofsly ignorant of, or you grofsly mifreprefent the motives of his parliamentary conduct. He patronized the militia bill, and and the Duke of Cumberland was no friend to it. This was the caufe of their mifunder-ftanding. He preferred the duty he owed his country to every other confideration, and dif-charged it faithfully, though the temporary difappointment of his military ambition, and the frowns of a prince, were to be the forfeit. When that prince difcountenanced a meafure fo congenial to the Englifh conftitution, he oppofed Mr. T——fh——d, not Mr. T——fh——d him.——As to the reft, I will not difturb the

little

little triumph of your fancy, but rather thank you for that play of words, which have led you from things to found, has spared me the trouble of an answer to an accusation too frivolous to deserve one.

There remain but two particulars more to be noticed, and then I shall follow you to a conclusion. L—d T——d's correction of Col. L—tt—l by a political bravo, is no less false than his launcing the thunder of a reversionary challenge at Dr. L——s. The mentioning Col. L—tt—l's name in the H. of Commons was merely accidental, and, from the circumstances of the time and the occasion, could not possibly have happened from suggestion or preconcert. It is in vain to refer you to all the members of the house who were present, for you knew the falsehood before you published it. As to the venerable infirm member, his own petulance drew upon him a reprimand which his vanity chose to interpret into a challenge, yet L—d T——d's words bore no such meaning, nor were so understood by any person present.

At your conclusion you labour hard in the affected strains of ungenuine pathetic, to give a mournful description of deceased merit at the expence of the living, and your impotence

seems

feems to encreafe in proportion to your efforts: *difeafe* and *death*, triumphs and lamentations, funeral obfequies, a venerable matron, fiends and heroes, Greeks and Romans, graves and monuments, are all grouped in the gloomy picture.

While the yet undecided fate of Canada and of a Britifh army were depending, the general who fucceeded to the command, had no leifure to cull fuch flowers of rhetoric to deck the grave of the departed conqueror; but, being himfelf a foldier, he paid a more judicious tribute to the merit of his colleague, by publicly teftifying that his intrepidity and fkilful operations had enfured the victory.

I muft fpend a few words more to detect another calumny, which has bafhfully retired from your text into an humble note, where you accufe him of ufurping General Monckton's province, and ignorantly or arrogantly figning the capitulation. After the death of General Wolfe, General Monckton was carried on board a fhip in the river, wounded, as it was thought mortally; and the command devolving upon Lord Townfhend, it was his duty and his province to fign the capitulation.

Having now done with your letter, allow me to fay a word or two to your perfon, and

to

to guess at your character by the marks of it in your composition.

You are not the friend of the community in general, for you wish to see all power engrossed by a few individuals: you are not the friend of Irish liberty, or of English government, for when you wish the tone of prerogative may never be relaxed, you wish it at the hazard of the people's affections and at the expence of the constitution of Ireland. Having told you what you are not, let me now tell you what you are. You are the friend of successful corruption, and an enemy to Lord Townshend, because he does not practise the art of corrupting. You are the admirer and humble imitator of Junius, and the fellow-labourer in the great harvest of sedition. The signature you have chosen is perhaps expressive of your disposition, take care that it may not be an omen of your catastrophe; since you would leave behind you, a reputation at best but infamously ambiguous;—to be resolved by your friends into an assassin, and by your enemies into a suicide.

March 3d, 1770.

Z   BROGHILL.

NUM-

NUMBER X.

Scis Proteu, ſcis ipſe; neque eſt te falۡlere cuiquam,
Sed tu deſine velle.   VIRG.

To J. P————Y, Eſq.

S I R,

ALTHOUGH the late rapid declenſion of your
importance, or, in the words of one of
your moſt ſubſervient devotees, " the piteous
" condition of a ſinking man, may ſeem to
" claim an exemption from the *freedom* of the
" preſent times, which ſpare none connected
" with public life ;"—— yet, as you have been
the principlal cauſe of that *freedom,* ſo injurious to many reſpectable characters, I think
myſelf at liberty, from facts which are in my
poſſeſſion, to continue my examination into
your conduct.

When greater duties are not neglected, (if
any can be greater) it is certainly no unworthy
occupation, to reſcue the reputations of good
men from the perſecutions of a licentious preſs
——that worſt, that *only* tyrant of the age we
live in ;——to ſtop, if poſſible, the tear which
your indelicate ſuggeſtions have forced down
the

the cheek of innocence; and to retort the
scandal on the most silly and presumptuous
demagogue, that ever attempted to govern a
kingdom.——Let me, also, teach the man,
whose ordinary private qualities have been so
long exaggerated into virtues, to apologized for
his public incapacity;——that to have retired
with gratitude and temper, when he *flung* up
the *reins*, had been the first and best service
he could have done his countrymen, and his
family.

There seems to be two confiderations, fir,
which have not been attended to, by those you
employ to arrange your materials against L——d
L———s, but which will naturally occur to
every reader who perufes your narrative, even
as a mere novel.——The firft is, What degree
of influence you could juftly claim over a
gentleman, who having supported you so many
years, is now pofleffed of an extenfive property, and powerful intereft, and, in that
fituation, owes at leaft fome attention to his
rank and public conduct. Doubtlefs he has
received marks of your friendfhip——yet ftill
you fhould recollect how amply you have
experienced, and profited by his support.
Here, furely, your advocates muft allow the
obligation reciprocal;——if not, produce, if
you

you can, one of thofe long lifts you annually
fpread before the Britifh adminiftration, and
with which you occafionally intimidated the C.
Governors here. I call on you, fir, to produce any one of thefe rolls of parliament,
wherein L——d L————s's family have not
ftood foremoft, as your ftrenuous friends and
fupporters, to whom you were already fo much
indebted for the uncommon power you held in
this kingdom, and might ftill have held, had
you beftowed upon, your friends a fair and
decent fhare of your confidence, and adhered
to that degree of moderation, you affected to
prefcribe to yourfelf. Thefe are truths, fir,
too well known for you to deny. Your peevifh,
ill-founded arrangements of others, has, in
fpite of their private affection, extorted a degree of juftification from them, which fully
confirms the very light opinion the world had
long entertained of your candour and love of
truth.

You had no more right to charge L——d
L————s with defertion, than the government
with feverity : the one you had long neglected,
the other you had always betrayed.—If you
will rank your fincereft advocates among your
hacks, and not refpect them as your friends ;
7   ——if

—if they are at be fummoned to a moment's warning, to drudge from the purpofes of men who have ever been your moft zealous opponents, and are to be marfhalled againft principles, by which your family have long ftood and flourifhed; give me leave to tell Mr. P——by, (though he be now the ftandard of Irifh independence) that he exacts an obedience which no liberal mind fhould either fubmit to, or require. Though you might term fuch a degree of proftitution, friendfhip, at the Conftitution Club, you would, fir, condemn it at the Caftle.

Had it pleafed nature to have beftowed on you one talent that could be deemed an ingredient for government, you had never preferred an infidious convention with orator F——d, to an honourable intercourfe with fo powerful a friend as L——d L——s; or the endlefs perplexities of Sir L——s O'B——n, to the punctual difcharge of the duties of your ftation.

I would farther enquire from your agents, what degree of fubmiffion, on public points, can alone fulfill L——d L——s's engagements to Mr. P——y? Is the maintaining a diftinction, which tends directly to a breach

be-

between the crown, and the people of this kingdom, to be the teſt of his gratitude?

In that caſe, L——d L———s would be both unfortunate and ſingular in his ſituation, if he was bound by a more implicit *allegiance* to Mr. P———y, than either that gentleman or his new ally, the D——e of L———r, acknowledge to the crown; from which they have received more obligations than any ſubject ſince the bigotted and capricious reign of James I.

As popularity ſeems now to be your firſt object, you may ſuppoſe it an excellent expedient to conciliate your injured friends, by imputing the late diſappointment of your *patriotic* projects, to L——d L———s; yet, be aſſured, ſir, it would have been ſome mark of wiſdom, to have ſubmitted patiently to a cataſtrophe, haſtened by your own want of principle and underſtanding;——and *then* to have reconciled yourſelf to retirement and obſcurity, for which your *genius* ſeems peculiarly adapted.

You have alledged, it ſeems, to palliate the deſerting from your friends, " my little bark " can no longer live in the ſtorm of the " preſent times; I can attend to nothing but " my own preſervation."——Be it ſo:——I do not wiſh to aggravate your diſtreſs, yet I know
not

not under what example you can find a fanction for your felfifhnefs. The Dutch mariner, 'tis true, abandons the veffel at the approach of danger, but the *captain* is the laft man who fteps into the fhallop:——you, fir, not only forfake the crew who embarked with you, but you leave them with imprecations; and when you fee them perifhing, your laft command is, not to accept of affiftance.

The world, fir, had fome reafon to expect a conduct more correfponding, even to the affec-tation of fuch focial qualities, as you pretend to;——nay, to your laft exhortations and pro-feffions to all around you, from the chair——A feries of abfurdities has now reduced you to the humiliating ftate of becoming a *retainer* of L———er houfe, and an abject fuppliant for a county addrefs at K——are, when neither your own perfonal weight, nor the rhetorical *menances* of your *falfe* ally, could procure that empty compliment at Kilkenny.

I am, fir, yours, &c.

May 4th, 1771

VERAX

NUM-

NUMBER XI.

Hi motus animorum, & hæc certamina tanta,
Pulveris exigui jactu compreſſa quiefcunt.

VIRG.

To JEOFFRY WAGSTAFFE, Efq.

SIR,

THE ignorance and perplexity of our
financiers might induce an unexperi-
enced perfon to think, that the national accounts depended on algebraic calculation ——
Every queftion propofed by adminiftration,
though clear and fimple in itfelf, is rendered
obfcure and unintelligible, by the harangues
of fome half-witted orators. The precifion
and pointed eloquence of Hutchinfon, cannot
refcue the Houfe from the endlefs perplexities
of Sir William M——y——re, and the obfcure
elaborate comments of Sir Lu——s O'B——n.
The candour and moderation of Mr. Malone;
his fuperior abilities, which never excited
envy, becaufe they were never exerted with

VOL. II.   H   un-

unmannered infolence, to obtain an ungenerous triumph over the weak and defencelefs:
——yet this diftinguifhed character cannot protect him from the illiberal invectives of the
Kilkenny orator, who feems determined to
make his countenance a true index to his
heart. The Attorney-General is juftly rewarded by his rhetorical client: perfonal abufe
is the coin with which Mr. F——d *fees* his
lawyers. Few men, perhaps, know mankind
better than Mr. T——ll; though he was de-
ceived in the orator, and is juftly punifhed for
his want of fagacity.

Laft Saturday's proceedings furnifh the
ftrongeft proof of the temper and principles of
our patriots——Procraftination and delay are
their objects. The fervants of the crown
agreed to every meafure which had the leaft
tendency to public utility——The arrears of
half-pay, and officers widows, were ftruck
off, and the only point in debate, was to
prevent any injuftice to *particulars*, which
might arife from this innovation.

To give the reader a clear idea of the fubject, I fhall infert a fhort abftract of the national account, as it *then* ftood.

Debt

	l.	s.	d.
Debt at Lady-day, 1771, by report of the Committee of Accounts,	788,474	11	4¼
To which was added, fo much difpofed of by addrefs of the Houfe of Commons, in feffion 1769, being a balance due from Mr. Prat, late deputy vice-treafurer,	17,994	1	5¾
Difmiffed collectors,	14,060	14	10⅝
	£820,529	7	7¼

£1094, a faving on the army, was deducted from the debt in the public accounts, by the Committee to whom they were referred.

Struck off.

	l.	s.	d.
Arrear of penfions,	2,514	8	4¼
——— of officers widows	24,237	5	1¼
——— of half-pay	11,457	14	1
	£ 38,209	7	7¼
	782,320	0	0¼
	£820,529	7	7¼
Funded debt remaining undrawn at Lady-day, 1771.	725,000	0	0

On

On this ground, the Attorney-General pro-posed the following resolution, " That the " debt of the nation at Lady-day, 1771, " amounted to the sum of 782,320l."

Mr. Huffey moved for another resolution, " That the *funded* debt of the nation at Lady-" day, 1771, only amounted to 725,000l." If this had paffed, the balance between the two sums, (57,320l.) which was unavoidably expended in fupport of his Majefty's govern-ment, would not be included in the national debt ;——and though every article of expence, which had occafioned the *exceedings* in the laft two years, had been already laid before the Committee of Accounts ; yet, if this abfurd motion had been carried in the affirmative, the Committee of Supply muft have *refolved* itfelf into a Committee of Accounts, to wrangle *once more* over thefe articles ! Numberlefs pre-cedents were produced, to fhew that the At-torney-General's motion was parliamentary and proper. The patriots, unable to anfwer their opponents arguments, moved for the queftion of adjournment, and divided upon it ; but finding every effort ineffectual, and that a fpirited majority were determined to do their duty, *they* at laft retired in defpair, and gave up the point.

I fhould

I fhould not omit mentioning a debate, which enfued on a refolution being propofed, for applying 9000l. to the credit of the nation. (returned in the arrears.) This was the remaining balance of a large fum, *appropriated* by act of parliament, to erect batteries for the fecurity and defence of the harbour of Corke, and to purchafe arms for the militia.

Lord Townfhend, it feems, in his tour through the fouthern parts of the kingdom, had obferved the prefent defencelefs ftate of the harbour of Corke. The money formerly granted, was *jobbed* away in building a fort and batteries, where they could be of no fervice. The fort has fallen into ruins, by the *firing of the guns on rejoicing days!*—yet there is an ifland in the mouth of the harbour, where batteries might be erected, which would in fome degree protect the trade of that opulent and commercial city. This idea his Excellency adopted—An eftimate had been made out, and it appeared, that the intended plan might be executed for 7500l. Mr. Ponfonby, the late Speaker, oppofed the meafure; very confiftently, indeed, becaufe it was not a jobb.——" He *talked* of 150,000l. being abfolutely " requifite for the work." His fon, one of the reprefentatives of the city of Corke, likewife exerted his hereditary eloquence againſt the eſſential intereſt of that city which had choſen him. Mr. F——d *digreſſed* in his uſual manner, and peremptorily inſiſted, " That " there was no occaſion for fortifications in " this kingdom, as he very well knew, that " France would never invade us. The idea " was prepoſterous and abſurd." To ſhew his " *ſkill* in geography, he ſaid, a French fleet " muſt ſail *up the Engliſh Channel*, and force " its way through the Britiſh fleet, in order to " land in the *ſouthern* or *weſtern* parts of this " kingdom !——That there was no reaſon to " believe that *Conflans* intended to land troops " on our coaſt, though *Thurot* (who was to " act in concert with him) had landed in the " North.——That he would never believe it.—— " That if the French intended to *ſtrike at the* " *vitals of our conſtitution*, they ſhould embark " at Calais, and land at Dover !"

You may think, Mr. Wagſtaffe, that I miſrepreſent his mode of reaſoning——I appeal to a numerous audience for the truth of what I advance. In ſhort, this celebrated orator often put me in mind of the BARBER's BOY, in the farce of the Upholſterer.

. Sir Lu——s O'B——n dropped his uſual grave and ſententious addreſs, and affected to be facetious.

cetious. Sir W. M——y——re was treated by
Mr. Scot, like the afs in the fable, for miftaking his talents, and mimicking the tricks of
a lap-dog; this gentle correction may be of infinite fervice to both thefe knights.

C——l B——rt——n fpoke in a manly, fpirited ftyle : his arguments were well received
by the Houfe, and had weight in deciding the
queftion.

I am, fir, yours,

November 26, 1771.

'Q   A SENATOR.

NUMBER XII.

Iratus Chremes, tumido delitigat Ore.   Hor.

To JEOFFRY WAGSTAFFE, Efq.

SIR,

DOCTOR Swift, in his " Short View of
the State of Ireland," includes the *non-
refidence* of a chief governor among the lift of
national grievances.——To remedy this, and
many other inconveniences, the celebrated Lord
Chatham, propofed a new political fyftem,
which was inftantly adopted, and happily

H 4   brought

brought to perfection by the prefent Lord
Lieutenant;—yet this very meafure has been
the caufe of all our complaints. The powerful ariftocracy which had fo long reigned without controul, could not be to relinquifh their
power; like pirates they immediately hung out
falfe colours, to deceive the people, and affemble them under the fpecious ftandard of patriotifm.—— To reftore *Independence* to the Houfe
of Commons has been reprefented as a defign
to enflave the nation. To attempt governing
the kingdom without Lords Juftices, was
efteemed high treafon aginft the conftitution.
The reverence ufually paid thofe mighty lords,
often made me recollect the cuftom of leading
an afs into church, and finging an anthem in
his praife; yet when Europe had emerged from
barbarifm, an attempt to abolifh this ridicu-
lous cuftom occafioned many riots among the
bigotted rabble.

The proceedings of the houfe furnifh the
ftrongeft proofs of thefe inveterate prejudices—
The nation is faid to be *bankrupt* and ruined,
finking under oppreffion, loaded with taxes,
curfed with a venal and corrupt adminiftration,
who profufely lavifh the public money in un-
neceffary expences. An honourable member,
who feems to have tuned his voice to the dole-

ful

ful notes of a paffing bell, lately preached a prolix funeral fermon over his country.—— Ireland was ruined becaufe——but I learn to imitate the Kilkenny orator, who fubftitutes virulent invective and perfonal defamation, for precifion in argument, and candor in debate. —Mr. H—ff—y's Attic elegance may apologize for his fatire;——but the premeditated joke, the forced conceit, the aukward raillery, are Mr. Flood's peculiarities, and diftinguifh him as much as *diftortion*, vociferation, and a *vicious* pronunciation, that would even difgrace the *Ciceronian* fociety.

After the ableft champions of *oppofition* had exbaufted their rhetoric, and exhibited their miftaken inaccurate calculations to gain the applaufe of the gallery, they were anfwered by the Prime Serjeant in a ftyle and manner that adds grace to a dry and tirefome fubject, and renders it agreeable. The patriots were fhewn to be weak reafoners and miferable financiers, and not in the leaft qualified for a feat at either the *old* or a *new* board. The inconfiftency of their argument was evident. In the year 1769—under Lord Townfhend's adminiftration, the trade of the kingdom it feems was annihilated, becaufe the revenue had decreafed £ 59,000.——Yet in 1761, un-

der the mild, wife, and œconomical Mr. P—
nf—by, a deficiency of £ 81,000 had spread
no alarm. The exports (our only beneficial
commerce) have encreased ;—yet if we were
to credit these fage politicians, the nation was
undone, becaufe the treafury was not enriched
by duties which arife on our imports. Thefe
new commercial principles are not to be found
in D'Avenant or Petty; the public fpirited
financiers may have picked them up from fir
W—ll—m M—yne, or—a writing mafter.

However, the debates yefterday in the houfe,
proved the legality and expediency of the New
Board, beyond a poffibility of doubt. The
Kilkenny orator, moved for the following refolution, " That the Houfe would not allow
" any fums applied to the payment of new Com-
" miffioners of Excife, but fhould credit the
" nation with their falaries." The illegality of
this motion was pointed out, as it was directly
contrary to a pofitive act of parliament, which
both empowered the king to appoint a New
Board; and alfo, provided for the additional
expence. Mr. F. then *modeftly* withdrew his
motion, and candidly apologized for intro-
ducing it, by acknowledging his ignorance
of the Excife Laws ! He then propofed another refolution, which was only a little defi-

2   cient

cient in fenfe and grammar: however, by the affiftance of Mr. Malone's judicious remarks, it was at laft reduced to Englifh, and fhaped into confiftency. The purport of it was, " that the Houfe would refufe their confent to " any alteration in the prefent Excife Laws, " which might carry into effect the divifion of the " Board, &c."——Mr. Mafon immediately perceived the abfurdity of agreeing to fuch a refolution, and to fhew it in the ftrongeft light, he propofed this amendment, " however *benefi-* " *cial* fuch an alteration might be for collect- " ing the public revenue." In the courfe of the debate, M. F. exhibited his ufual oratorial powers: he compared the friends of Government to a PHALANX, which penetrated like a WEDGE through the loofe ranks of independence.——Metaphors, and figurative expreffions, introduced with elegance and propriety have a *peculiar* beauty; But Mr. F——d defpifes fuch *puerilities:* his inaccuracies, his blunders, his miftakes, are owing to the fublimity of his genius: he refembles the ancient philofopher who often fell into a ditch, while he was ftudying aftronomy, and contemplating the ftars. ——Even Potter's Antiquities might teach him to diftinguifh between a PHALANX and a WEDGE, and not ufe thefe terms as *fynonymous,* in a finished oration. However, as Mr. F. seems *angry* at a friendly hint you formerly gave him, to vary his studies from Demosthenes to Salmon's Grammar, I shall say no more on the subject.

Sir George Macartney, in a sensible manly tone of reasoning, defended the measures of administration. M. F. had asserted, " that it was an indignity and insult offered the House, to appoint a New Board, in contradiction and defiance of their *. late resolution.*" Sir George proved, how inexplicit, indecisive, and nugatory, this boasted resolution was; it was entirely *retrospective*, and could not by any construction *extend* to the *future*. He justly termed it an *inuendo* resolution. It was neither addressed to the King, or the Lord Lieutenant. The House ordered the Speaker to lay it before his Excellency, and he told them he would transmit it to his Majesty; but at the same time informed them, he had received his Majesty's orders for dividing the Boards.

Though he gave the House that information, they still hoped the King would *recal* or *cancel* those letters. For it is universally believed, that the patriots chief objections were

* That seven Commissioners had *hitherto* been sufficient.

not

not grounded on the inexpediency of the meafure, but arofe from *perfonal* pique and difappointment. They could not bear to think,
that gentlemen, who had fupported government, and acted wifely, fhould be diftinguifhed by their fovereign's favour, when fome of
their leaders had been difmiffed for folly and
ingratitude: the contraft was too ftrong and
humiliating.————They alfo had another excellent reafon for oppofing the prefent arrange-
ment.——As they *probably* intend fupporting a
future adminiftration, they meant to keep the
New Board as a referve, to be compofed of
their friends, and therefore cannot forgive Lord
Townfhend, for cutting off this *dernier re-
fource.*

It is evident to a demonftration, that Mr.
P———nf———by's chief aim was to eftablifh
a new board for the provifion of his friends.
In his virtuous adminiftration, and in the
firft year of his prefent Majefty's reign, *the* act
paffed, which has facilitated the execution of
this long projected fcheme, *fanctioned* by three
particular acts of parliament.——The expence at
the utmoft will not exceed 12,000l. per ann.——
and the gain to the revenue will probably be
five times as much; for it is well known, that
the inland excife of Ireland is now lefs than it

was

was a century ago; and yet the people, and consequently the consumption, is nearly doubled.

. No one exclaimed so loudly against the expence of the board as the œconomical Mr. J———n P———ns———by. He *prophesied* it would occasion a land tax, (which he has taken care his tenants must pay) and also, that the measure itself was impracticable, without a new clause in the act.——It is really pleasant to observe this gentleman in his new character of an œconomist——The man who had for so many years loaded the country with unnecessary sine-cures——he who had swelled the charges of the revenue in incidents and sallaries, from 69,651l. 15s. 2d. to 114,714l. 4s. 3d. annually.——This insidious management of the revenue rendered government dependent on the Irish aristocracy: consequently the patriotic prostitution of it, became a fundamental maxim in their politics. New taxes were levied on the people to supply the deficiency ; and the odium was thrown on government, by these *conscientious* gentlemen.

When Mr. P———ns———by presided at the Board, Capt. Mercer was permitted to build as many boats as he pleased. He built one, called the Hibernia, for Mr. Glover. Her *outset* cost 4000l. Her annual expence was 6000l.

6000l. though she never made a capture. When Mr. Beresford, and sir W. Osborne, were appointed Commissioners, they thought it their duty to enquire into the matter. They found she was totally unfit for any purpose. To make an experiment, however, they ordered her to block up the port of Rush; she did so; at low water, the smugglers all sailed out, the *Hibernia* was lying dry, and could not float 'till high water. Captain M—r—er, on being examined, was obliged to give in a report in writing, that she was unserviceable. Here was a *dead* expence of 4000l. incurred at first, besides 6000l. per annum; which is above half the sum the new board can possibly cost. This is *only* one example of Mr. P—nf—by's œconomy.

The last motion proposed in the H—fe, could only proceed from a head stored with such *trumpery* ideas, as Mr. B—ry B—ry's. " that the Commissioners of the Excise, should " be suspended from their functions in parlia- " ment." This motion was treated with cold contempt. Mr. Bushe's arguments on the sub- ject, were masterly, spirited, and ingenious. This Mr. Wagstaffe, was the last effort of Mr. P. and an expiring faction; of a faction whose last efforts against the establishment of a

new

new board, may be compared to the convulſive ſtruggles of a *headleſs* fly, that ſeems for a moment to acquire ſtrength from the very wound that deſtroys it.

Yours, &c.

February 15th, 1772.

Q   SENATOR.

NUMBER XIII.

Et ſermone opus eſt, modo triſti, ſæpe jocoſo.
HOR.

To JEOFFRY WAGSTAFFE, Eſq.

SIR,

I Obſerve with concern, that you entertain the public on ſubjects of national importance, ſeldomer than uſual. 'Tho' ridicule has not the weight of ſerious argument, yet, perhaps, you ſuppoſe it more embarraſſing to your patriotic antagoniſts; like MARIUS's javelins, which by breaking and ſticking in the enemies ſhields, contributed more to his victory over the Gauls, than ſtronger and more piercing weapons.

You

You have taken no notice of the moſt judicious and beſt calculated bill for the improvement of the revenue; the eaſe of the ſubject,
and the benefit of the fair trader, that was ever
introduced into the Houſe of Commons.   The
very objections to this bill proved its utility.
It is ſcarcely credible; ſir, that thoſe gentlemen, who in the beginning of the ſeſſion, complained ſo loudly of the heavy expence of *New
Boards,* and of the deficiency of the revenue,
ſhould make its *eventual* increaſe, the grounds
of their oppoſition.   The clauſe, " contained
" in an act paſſed in the 14th and 15th Charles
" II, which entitled our merchants to a draw-
" back of ſix pence a gallon, on rum firſt
" landed in England," was evidently deſigned
to reſtrain our commerce, by preventing a direct communication with America.   About
the year 1757, the merchants firſt diſcovered
and availed themſelves of this clauſe, which
reduced the revenue above 50,000l. per annum.   This is an experimental proof of the
utility of repealing it : beſides, it will induce
our merchants to trade directly with America,
without uſing the medium of England. The
great trading city of Corke, has already ex-
preſſed its approbation of this judicious meaſure, equally beneficial to our commerce and
finances.

Let us now examine the weighty arguments urged against repealing this clause. " By an " encreafe of the hereditary revenue, fays Mr. " F. the crown may fupport the civil and mi- " litary eftablifhments, without the aid of the " additional duties; and confequently the ab- " folute necefity of calling frequent parlia- " ments will ceafe." This reafoning neither fpecious, nor folid, is eafily refuted. The ut- moft encreafe of the revenue, by every judi- cious regulation introduced into the new bill, cannot exceed 100,000l. on the higheft compu- tation. The loan for the current fervice of two years, is 200,000l. Even fuppofing that 100,000l. will be fufficient next feffion, the *expected rife* in the revenue, will juft fupply the (otherwife unavoidable) deficiency, and prevent the prejudicial increafe of the national debt. But our patriots ufe every art to deceive the public, by mifreprefenting the true and ob- vious tendency of every ufeful regulation, a- dopted by the fervants of the crown. Thofe gentlemen feem confcious of the badnefs of their caufe, and pay an involuntary compli- ment to the prefent adminiftration, by fubfti- tuting fubtlety and obfcurity in their arguments; inftead of perfpicuity and precifion; as fhop- keepers darken their windows, to fcreen the damaged

damaged *goods*, which they expofe to fale, from too ftrong a light.——The candid and impartial are now convinced, that the late deficiencies in the revenue, may be rationally accounted for, without recurring to that patriotic origin of every diftrefs—the prorogation ! Let us leave that ftale and hacknied *folution* to a fet of men, who by a ftrange affociation of ideas cannot declaim on the national grievances or calamities without the aid of this popular topic ; as the young gentleman mentioned by Mr. Locke, could not dance without the affiftance of an old trunk, placed in a corner of his room.

The claufe inferted in the revenue bill, to prevent all perfons from keeping twelve gallon ftills in their houfes, except for medicinal waters, or experiments in chemiftry, will prove the beft check on the great confumption of fpirituous liquors, which ruin both the health and morals of the lower ranks of people. Sir W——m Of——b——ne afferted, that there were at leaft five thoufand ftills in the kingdom, which furnifhed four hundred thoufand gallons of whifkey at a reduced price, as *it* paid no excife, by which the crown and the fair trader were equally injured.

Nothing could be more frivolous than what fell from fome of our celebrated orators

on

on this subject.　They confidered man in the abstract, " as a being intitled to diftil whifkey, " and drink it without being reftrained by the " laws of civil fociety, which are an arbitrary " encroachment on the rights and privileges of " the fubject."　By a parity of reafoning, all mankind fhould be again reduced to their original condition, and the fteps taken by government, to fupprefs the northern infurgents, (though folicited by the felf-conftituted affertors of liberty) may be deemed an infraction of the Magna Charta of nature.　However, *that* reftriction was at laft adopted by a confiderable majority.　It is to be hoped, fir, that we fhall foon fee our finances flourifh under a refident Vice-roy, and jobbing banifhed from every department of the ftate..　The many excellent acts introduced into the Houfe this feffion, to regulate our interior police, and provide for our domeftic fecurity, when paffed into laws, and ftrictly executed, may be the happy means of civilizing a country, not yet wholly emerged from barbarifm.　　：

The people, taught by experience, and repeated examples, will no longer confide in a fet of fallacious patriots, whom Mr. Sc——tt juftly compared to deceiving empirics, who both create *the difeafe, and live by it*.　They will

judge

judge of the conduct of their reprefentatives on fixed principles. They will be afhamed to reverence the fame man in the character of a patriot, whom they lately execrated as a courtier; like the ignorant devotees at Rome, who now worfhip Jupiter, by the name of St. Peter, and cling round his knees with devotion, fince he has been baptized and converted by the Pope, from a Heathen image into a Chriftian Saint.

I am, fir, yours,

March 21ft, 1772.

A SENATOR.

NUMBER XIV.

La regie, eft l'adminiftration d'un bon pere de famille, qui leve lui même avec économie, & avec ordre fes revenus. L'ESPRIT des LOIX.

To JEOFFRY WAGSTAFFE, Efq.

SIR,

IT is a cuftom among the Dutch, to burn a great quantity of their imported fpices, in order to enhance the value of the remaining part, by producing an artificial fcarcity. Mr. P——nf——by certainly acted on the fame princi-

ple

ple (when he was premier) in sinking the hereditary revenue, and reducing government to the necessity of giving his friends and dependents an advanced price for their votes.——The Revenue-bill, sir, tho' replete with so many wise and just regulations, was obstinately, and violently opposed by him, and all those who are subject to implicit obedience, by servilely acting under their selfish and ambitious leaders.

At the beginning of this session, the pernicious tendency of the projected loan, was displayed in all the glowing colours of oratory. It was prophesied in the desponding accents of despair, that " it would ruin this impoverished, " distressed, exhausted country, by drawing " the cash out of the traders hands, and throw- " ing it into the funds." Now, when a rational scheme, pregnant with national advantage is proposed, the cry is changed ; " the " crown will be rendered independent, and " no more parliaments will be held in this " kingdom." Yet, if the rise in the revenue answers our most sanguine expectations, *it* will only preclude the necessity of *involving us more in debt.*——Mr. F. ingeniously observed, " that the establishment of two *useless boards,* " might now become *public benefits,* as they " would prevent a *redundancy* in the treasury,

" *which*

" *which* might overturn the constitution." —
That gentleman poſſeſſes the peculiar art of in-
ſpiring his friends with a coincidence of ſentiment. They unanimouſly agreed with him in
the juſtneſs of his obſervation, and are now determined to accept of *new places*, the firſt opportunity ; ſince that great caſuiſt and politi-
cian has convinced them, that they may promote the welfare of their country, by gratify-
ing their own inclinations.

Let us now examine what has been the chief
object of Iriſh patriotiſm ?—To reduce his
Majeſty's revenue, and to compel the King's
repreſentative to buy off the oppoſition of a
few turbulent and buſy men, who, whilſt they
hold out ſpecious profeſſions of attachment to
their ſovereign's perſon and government, were
ſtriking at the very *means* of his eſtabliſhment,
and involving him and his people in one common diſtreſs. Happily for this country, a re-
ſident Vice-roy has at laſt checked that pernicious ſyſtem of policy, which ſo long actuated
the *Iriſh cabinet.*

It may be uſeful here to ſubmit a few obſer-
vations to the candid reader, on the fallacious
reaſoning which has been artfully employed to
miſrepreſent the true and obvious tendency of
the clauſe, inſerted in the act to continue the
Revenue-

Revenue-bill, from June, 1774, *to the end of the then next seffion of parliament.* The gentlemen in oppofition have faid, " that if the " crown did not think proper to call a parlia- " ment at the *ufual time,* the hereditary reve- " nue might be collected by this bill, though " the additional duties would ceafe." This is not a fact ;——for the only part of the hereditary revenue included in the act, is the *licences,* and the *moiety* of tobacco feized ; confequently *that* bill has for *its* immediate, and principal object, the *additional duties ;* and as they are *only* granted from feffion to feffion, the power of the commons over *the national purfe* would ftill remain in full force, though the claufe had made *that* act perpetual. The Revenue-bill derives its chief weight and efficacy (in refpect to the crown) from the act which grants his Majefty the *additional duties,* and without them it would be almoft nugatory.

The *prerogations* in 1753, and 1769, were likewife held up, *in terrorem,* by our declaiming orators ; and it was plaufibly urged, " that " limiting the bill to four years, would be a " proper check on *that* invidious branch of the " prerogative." Sir William Ofborne, with his ufual knowledge and precifion, expofed the futility of this argument, by obferving that the

acts

acts which granted the hereditary revenue to
Charles II. had also provided for the collection
of it. By the old book of rates, our Weſtern
exports paid three per cent. though at preſent
they do not pay above *one*. By the *Revenue-
bill*, the duties on all ſtuffs uſed for bleaching
and dying, are taken off;—new regulations
adopted, to encourage our ſtaple manufacture,
and additional duties impoſed on all foreign
linen. By Sir William's judicious and ſolid
remarks, it was evident to the candid and impartial, that the *public* alone could ſuffer if the
act expired; as the hereditary revenue would
rather be *increaſed*, and the crown rendered *more*
independent. How abſurd, *then*, was it to ſuppoſe, that a limitation of the bill to *four years*
could operate as a check on the prerogative?

If a conteſt between the executive power,
and the commons, ſhould *again* occaſion a prorogation, who would wiſh to ſee the commerce
and manufactures of the kingdom eſſentially
injured, by not inſerting a clauſe, which is
chiefly calculated for the eaſe and benefit of the
ſubject, and the extenſion of commerce?——
The apprehenſion of this might damp the ſpi-
rited efforts of our patriots in the cauſe of freedom, and induce them to accept of a Money-
bill, *originated* in the council, *agreeable to Poyn-*

ings' law!——Thus, fir, the conftitutional independence of the commons is fecured by that
very obnoxious claufe; without it, they might
be induced, through pity and compaffion, to
facrifice their *legal privileges* for the fake of the
people.

Ever fince the year 1726, *that* claufe has
been conftantly inferted; the *rejection* of it
muft have been deemed an *innovation*. Certainly, fir, it is not treating his majefty with
the refpect and confidence he deferves, to
throw out malicious infinuations, and manifeft
an unjuft and groundlefs fufpicion of him.
The Englifh miniftry, in feveral inftances,
have proved themfelves friends to the true intereft of this kingdom. To conciliate the favour of government, by all *proper means*, is
true policy, and fhould be the aim of every
honeft man, who is neither *fervile* nor *factious*.
If our patriots, by their late conduct, fhould
acquire the favour and efteem of the public,
I would exclaim with furprize, like the Spar-
tan who caught his *deformed*, difgufting wife,
in bed with her gallant: " Wretched man,"
fays he, " what dire neceffity could drive
" thee to this! '

I am, fir, yours,

A Senator.

Q

NUMBER XV.

Judiciorum defiderio, tribunitia poteftas effiagitata eft:
  judiciorum levitate, ordo quoque alius ad res judi-
  candas poftulatur. Judicium culpa atque dedecore,
  etiam cenforium nomen, quod afperius antea populo
  videri folebat, id nunc pofcitur : id jam populare,
  atque plaufibile factum eft.

CICERONIS Oratio pro L. Muræna.

To JEOFFRY WAGSTAFFE, Efq.

SIR,

LAST Saturday I attended the debates in
the houfe of commons, on J—ge R——n's
conduct. Their fpirited and liberal proceedings deferve the higheft applaufe. Moderation,
candour, and impartiality diftinguifhed the
Speaker : he fhewed himfelf (what he has always been) a ftrenuous friend to liberty, and a
determined opponent to every fpecies of op-
preffion. His profound knowledge in the laws
and conftitution of his country, conveyed in a
manly ftrain of commanding eloquence, diffi-
pated every doubt, and ftruck conviction to
every heart. Mr. P——ry appeared like a
Hampden or Hollis, afferting the rights of the
fubject, againft the arbitrary and illegal mea-

fures, fanctioned by venal prerogative lawyers, who meanly proftituted themfelves to a tyrannical court. ——Mr. F——d's impetuous eloquence, grounded on the firm bafis of truth and juftice, captivated the paffions, and convinced the understanding.——Counfellor Fitz———ns, in the true fpirit of his *prefent*, and *original* profeffion, attempted to anfwer their arguments with his ufual fophiftry;——a ftranger to the precifion and difcriminating judgment of a Malone, he fubftitutes in their room evafive quibbles, and *diftinctions* without a *difference*. This venerable patriot's virtue and confiftency are apparent: he exerts himfelf to vindicate an unjuft judge; but is too confcientious to fupport an honeft and difinterefted adminiftration. He acts like *that* virtuous pope who firft ordained celibacy among the clergy; yet, to palliate the feverity of his injunction, indulged the priefts with concubines inftead of wives.

If J——ge R——n had flourifhed in the reign of a Charles, or a James, *principles* fo congenial to his royal mafter's, muft have met with fuitable encouragement. Amongft the various oppreffive modes of levying money on the fubject, without the confent of parliament, *his* would have been adopted and cherifhed. What better expedient could be devifed, than to fine a county, a county, *ad libitum*, for a pretended neglect in not repairing a road? for it muſt be admitted, that if a judge preſumes to *determine*, without *proper* information, and *legal* evidence, it is not material whether his deciſion be founded on a *fact* or not. Even if the right of fining a county for not repairing a *turn-pike* road was clearly eſtabliſhed, yet ſome deference ſhould be paid to a ſet of gentlemen, and a reſpectable body of freeholders; they ſhould be liſtened to, calmly and diſpaſſionately, to hear what they could alledge, either to palliate or apologize for the omiſſion. But this arrogant and ignorant man ſeems to have borrowed his maxims of juriſprudence from ſome of the Turkiſh baſhaws, who firſt condemn and execute the ſuppoſed criminal, and then graciouſly indulge his friends with leave to commence a proteſs, and give proofs of his innocence.

I own, Mr. Wagſtaffe, I was aſhamed to obſerve ſuch ſtrong marks of prejudice among the gentlemen of the long robe, in favour of Mr. R——n. Were they induced to ſympathize with a worthleſs individual of their fraternity, by a conſcious ſimilarity of ſentiment? or, perhaps, they would not chooſe to abridge the power of a judge, however arbitrary or il-

legal, as *they* live in patient expectation of being exalted, to the bench. It is somewhat remarkable, that lawyers and taylors are ever moft
zealous for the *honour* of their profeffion : the
reafon affigned for this peculiarity is too invidious for me to mention. The fuperior abilities of a Perry, a Malone, and a Hutchifon,
may preferve them from the epidemic taint of
the *profeffion*. But an exception which arifes
from *fingular* circumftances, cannot operate
againft a general and well eftablifhed maxim.

What wretched arguments were Mr. R——n's
advocates obliged to adopt? The conftitutional right of the reprefentatives of the people,
to examine and cenfure the conduct of our
judges, was queftioned.——How often has this
inherent privilege been exercifed for the public
good? We fhould gratefully remember, that
what are *now* courts of law, would have been
courts of inquifition ; and the judges ftate in-
quifitors, without the generous efforts of the
commons. When the chofen delegates of the
people execute their truft with fpirit and fide-
lity, judicial proceedings will be conducted on
the principles of equity and unfophifticated
reafon.——Various attempts have been made
by the reverend fages of the bench, to *refine*
away the undoubted right of juries, to judge

of

of both *law* and *fact*: this Star-Chamber doctrine has never wanted advocates; and it is well-known that the lawyers, to a man, have always opposed the reform of abuses, or any attempt to make the forms of law more confonant to the dictates of common fenfe. " Brufh down a fingle cobweb in Weftmin- " fter-Hall," faid Lord Chatham, " and the " old fpider will crawl out."

There is a fhameful indolence and fupine- nefs too prevalent among Irifhmen. A nation that enjoys *few* privileges, fhould be tenacious of thofe they have; yet it required the utmoft exertion of Mr. F———d's abilities, to roufe the country gentlemen, and make them fenfi- ble of the importance of the fubject. Mr. R———n, to aggravate his offence, had treated the houfe with contempt, by neither *attending*, or deigning to fend any meffage, or authoriz- ing any of his friends to apologize for his vicious conduct: he had prefumptuoufly acted in defiance of MAGNA CHARTA, and through paffion and ignorance, made a breach in the conftitution, contrary to his duty and oath. *His* principles are uniform and confiftent. He makes no fcruple of facrificing the rights of the fubject to whim and caprice; and the life of a wretched criminal, to pique and refentment.

I fhall

I fhall produce two anecdotes, well authenticated, to fupported my affertion. Some years
ago, when Mr. R———n went the circuit, he
was a little difcompofed by the jolting of the
carriage : in a rage, he exclaimed, " that he
" would fine the county." His brother judge
calmly obferved, " that the road did not run
" through any part of his circuit." Mr. R.
ftill infifted " that he would fine the county
" not as a judge of affize, but as one of the
" juftices of the King's Bench, for in that
" capacity, his jurifdiction extended to all
" parts of the kingdom."——The fecond inftance happened in a neighbouring county : he
had recommended it to a jury to reprefent a
perfon capitally convicted before him for horfe-
ftealing, as an object of mercy. However,
they did not pay due attention to his recommendation. After the judge had returned from his
circuit, the criminal had given fome ufeful information, and difcovered feveral of his accom-
plices : induced by thefe confiderations, the
gentlemen of the grand jury wrote in his favour to Mr. R———n, and defired that he
would reprefent the criminal's cafe to government. But this righteous judge refufed to
comply with *their* requeft, thought it coincided
with his former fentiments, *becaufe* the jury
had

had not *implicitly* obeyed his mandate; and so the poor wretch fell a victim to his obstinacy.

I question whether the Persian judge, who was flead by Cambyses, and his skin stuffed, to serve instead of a *wool pack* for his successors, had not more compassion and humanity than this servile copier of a Scrogs or Jeffries. For my part, I hope the house will address his Majesty to remove him from the bench; for such a judge is a disgrace and insult to a free country. Mr. R———n will be little affected by what I can say: callous to those nice feelings which are ever inseparable from the least degree of genius, he wraps himself up in pride and dullness. Nature has endued *such* men with self-conceit, which increases in a *direct ratio* to the contempt and scorn with which they are treated, as fish are endued with swim-bladders, that expand and buoy them up in proportion to the depth of water in which they are immersed.

I am, sir, yours,

March 3, 1772.

ALFRED.

NUM-

NUMBER XVI.

To JEOFFRY WAGSTAFFE, Efq.

SIR,

WHEN faction and difappointed ambition, appear under the fpecious difguife of public fpirit, we fhould always appeal to facts, to judge of the conduct of government. Satire and invective, on *either* fide, only fhew the wit and ingenuity of the writer, but *prove nothing*. The cry of liberty, and the profeffion of Roman zeal to defend the rights and liberties of the people, when they are in no danger, often render the integrity of our patriots juftly problematical. They refemble our modern quacks, who are always recommending the virtue and efficacy of their medicines, and modeft advertifements, to impofe on the ignorant and credulous.

It is an incontrovertible fact, that the linen manufacture is our ftaple commodity; confequently, its extenfion and improvement merits the principal attention of every Chief Governor, who interefts himfelf in the profperity of Ireland.

Ireland. By this criterion let us judge of
Lord Townshend's administration. ————

It must be allowed, Mr. Wagstaffe, that
the bounty granted by England, on the exportation of Irish linen, has enabled us to
carry that manufacture to its present perfection. This bounty was first granted in the
year 1742; and in a few years the number of
yards exported gradually encreased from six to
12,891,318 yards, value 751,993l.——In 1751,
the bounty expired. In 1752, the exports de-
creased 2,235,315 yards;—— loss to Ireland,
130,393l.

Various attempts were made, but without
success, for a renewal of this bounty, till the
year 1756,

The exports *then*

11,944,328 yds.——value 796,288l.

In 1757, when the bounty took place,
15,508,709 yds.——value 1,033,931l.

Increased in exports,

3,564,381 yds.——value 237,625l.

In the year 1744, the quantity of Irish linen
receiving bounty, was 2,100,000 yards. In
1750, 3,400,000 yards. It now exceeds five
millions.——It must give every friend to his
country, the most sincere pleasure to observe

I 6

the

the present flourishing state of our linen manufacture. I shall lay before the reader, our exports for the three last years.

In the year 1769, ——— 17,790,705 yards.

In the year 1770, ——— 20,560,754 yards.

In the year 1771, ——— 25,376,805 yards.

The bounty paid on the exportation of British and Irish linens, for thirteen years and a half, amounted to 492,153l. 6s. 7d. The medium this year was 45,257l. of which 23,130l. to Ireland, and 22,497l. to Great Britain——. Let every Irishman remember, that we are indebted to Lord T————d for a *renewal*, and an *addition* to this bounty, in the year 1770.

Mr. Grenville afferts, that the " Exports " from Ireland to the British colonies, have " encreafed fince the peace, upon a medium " of five years, 101,702l." We may depend on this calculation, as Mr. Bourke paffes it by *unnoticed* in his *accurate Obfervations on the State of the Nation.* Though Mercator's remarks may be juft, " That the linen trade declined " foon after the late peace," yet that check was but momentary ; our encreafed exports to America, fince that period, prove beyond a possibility of doubt, that our ftaple manufacture was never in a more flourifhing ftate.

In

In the year 1769, the Manchester manufacturers presented a petition (supported by Lord Strange, and sir George Saville) for a bounty of three half-pence a yard on all checks. If this petition had been carried, it would have ruined our linen manufacture, by operating as a bounty of 45l. per cent. against it ;— for every one conversant in busines knows, that Manchester is supplied with Irish yarn, and that our home manufacture is essentially injured by the large exportation of yarn from Derry, Drogheda, and other ports. What would have been our situation in a short time, if this scheme had succeeded?——In the committee, the petition was rejected by *only* a majority of *one*. The measure, at that time, was prevented by his Excellency's care and vigilance.

In the year of 1770, another petition was presented by the Manchester manufacturers. An application was then made by the Linen-board to the Lord Lieutenant, and a memorial drawn up on the subject. Mr. A———n was instantly dispatched to England, and by his comprehensive knowledge of our linen trade, he was enabled to set the matter in so strong and clear a light, that the attempt *again* failed of success.——It is well known, that his Excellency personally interested himself in this affair, and

and by his affiduity, and ftrenuous reprefentations to the Englifh miniftry, and by private letters to his particular friends, he obtained fuch an influence in the Englifh houfe, that our linen trade was preferved from ruin, and the bounty on Englifh checks limited to an halfpenny per yard.

It is evident, Mr. Wagftaffe, that an extenfion of our trade depends on the favour of Great Britain : the people of England, in general, are extremely jealous, and are perpetually foliciting the commons for bounties, which indirectly ftrike at the ftaple commodity of this kingdom.——We are indebted to the miniftry, and the friendly aid of our Chief Governor, for preventing the intended blow : it is, therefore, our duty and intereft to act on conciliating principles, and not raife a violent clamour on trifles, merely from perfonal and felfifh motives. If our patriots act on public-fpirited principles, let them abolifh that difgraceful privilege, which diftinguifhes them from their fellow-fubjects, and exempts m——rs of p————nt from the obligation of acting like *honeft men.*

To provide a maintenance for the indigent, and force thofe to work who are a burthen to the community, would remove a national difgrace : our ftreets and roads are filled with objects

objects that excite both horror and compassion. A relaxation of the penal laws would *enrich*, improve, and and prevent the depopulation of this country. Beggary and luxury are feen here in exftremes. To revive trade in the capital, is not fufficient; nor will fuch a narrow fuftem of policy be of effential fervice. A paralytic perfon may have warmth at the heart, though the extremities are cold and fenfelefs.——Hibernia, in its prefent ftate, might be exhibited like Anfon's failors, "who "dreffed themfelves in the laced and embroi- "dered cloaths of the Spaniards, and put them "on over their own dirty trowfers and jackets."

I am, fir, yours,

Y   A Merchant.

N U M B E R XVII.

O fortunatis nimium, fua fi bona norint.   Virg.

To Jeoffry Wagstaffe, Efq.

SIR,

CRANTZ, in his hiftory of Greenland, defcribes "a kind of fifh, that has a "large head, and eyes like an owl; the "Green-

" Greenlanders call them *Ingeminiſet*, becauſe
" they growl when they dive down."——Our
patriots bear a ſtriking reſemblance to this
fiſh : with viſages diſtorted by envy, diſappointment, and *affected* grievances, they *groan
in ſpirit*, from their retreats, and inſidiouſly
attempt to infuſe their own gloomy ideas
into their countrymen.

The deficiency of the revenue has furniſhed
ample field for patriotic declamation, though
it may be eaſily proved, that the balance of
trade in our favour, is *proportionate* to this
very deficiency; for the revenue ariſes from
the duties on our imports, which chiefly
conſiſt of foreign luxuries ;—— conſequently,
national commerce (by which I mean our export trade) may be in a flouriſhing ſtate, when
our revenue is at the loweſt ebb. The ab-
ſurdity then of ſuch logic and complaints,
muſt appear evident to the unprejudiced and
impartial.

Our patriots, indeed, can readily diſcover
the ſource of all our misfortunes. A decay
of trade, bankruptcies, poverty and idleneſs,
are all originated by the baneful influence of
government :——thoſe ingenious gentlemen offer
an eaſy ſolution 'for every difficulty. The
proteſt and prorogation were long held out to

the

the ignorant multitude as the fole canfe of the dearnefs of corn, and high price of provifions. Such profound politicians reafon like Lapland philofophers, who fay when it thunders, "that two women are ftretching and flap-"ping a dried feal-fkin, and the thunder pro-"ceeds from that rattle."

I think it might be eafily demonftrated, not-withftanding all our complaints of the op-preffion and injuftice of England, that we have ftill ample refources within ourfelves ;—that we might extend our trade, and improve our agriculture, if our nobility and gentry had *public spirit*, and our manufacturers honefty and induftry. The extortion and rack-rents of our landlords depopulate and ruin the kingdom. Every neteffary of life is as dear in Dublin, as in London, though we have not the thoufandth part of its commerce, opulence, or circulating fpecie.—Some years fince, we carried on an advantageous, though clandeftine trade with Spain and Portugal, by annually exporting camblets and ftuffs to the value of 300,000l. This we have loft, by *falfe package*, and other frauds and impofitions. We even fee that neither the affiduity and care of the Legiflature, nor the laudable zeal and vigilance of the Linen-board, can effec-

tually

tually suppress the scandalous practice of frau-
dulent lapping, and other mean cheats so
universally complained of, in our linen manufacture.

Till some vigorous measures are adopted, to
check the illegal combination of our workmen,
it will always be in the power of a set of
drunken, disorderly fellows, to blast every judicious and beneficial scheme for the improvement
of our manufactures and extension of our commerce.——A strong instance of this appears in an
excellent pamphlet, entitled, "An address to
"the Representatives of the People." "A few
"years ago," says this sensible writer, "we
"had some expectations of gaining a little
"foreign trade for ready-made shoes, and I
"think præmiums were given by the Dublin
"Society to the exporters. Hence we were flat-
"tered with the hopes of this becoming a branch
"of some little profit to the nation, since every
"pair of shoes that should be exported, would
"be a clear gain to the kingdom: but this
"hope was destroyed in its bud. The journey-
"men shoe-makers turned out for wages, and
"the masters remained stiff for three weeks or
"a month, in so much, that the public were
"in great distress for shoes, even that several
"were under the necessity of sending to Lon-
"don

" don for them, and still continue to do so,
" alledging, that they can be supplied sooner,
" cheaper, and better than in Dublin.—At
" length, terms were made, and the journey-
" men's wages advanced four-pence a pair upon
" men's shoes, so in proportion for women's
" and children's. This was a tax upon the
" public, which, although submitted to at
" home, might, and I believe has lost the little
" share of foreign trade we were in expectation
" of. But the imposition did not stop here ;—
" because the journeymen raised their price
" four pence a pair for men's shoes, the mas-
" ters very modestly at once, raised the price
" upon the public a *shilling*, or *eighteen pence* a
" pair, which is from 200 to 350 per cent.
" on the journeymen's advance. Leather they
" have said was dear——raw hides are fallen
" cent. per cent. but I do not hear of shoes
" falling in price.——Thus, one example fol-
" lows another, and mechanics in almost every
" branch of business, in their turns, form
" combinations for an advance of wages ;
" merely, I fear, that the earning of three
" days a week, may enable them to spend the
" other four in the ale-house."

Truths of this sort, Mr. Wagstaffe, that
" come home to men's business and bosoms,"

may

may have a good effect on some of your readers, and succeeded better than a gentler address.

I shall conclude my letter with another extract from the same pamphlet, as it has an immediate connection with our present subject.

" The capital articles *not exportable*, and " which at present seem to monopolize the " zealous attention of the public, are

" The silk manufacture,

" The woollen manufacture.

" Those exportable are, —— Linen, corn, " tallow, wool, beef, butter, pork, hides, " fish dried, &c.

" These articles, circumstanced as *we are*, I " conceive, should reduce the attention of this " kingdom to two grand objects,

" AGRICULTURE and LINEN : Fish may be " added.

" The branches of agriculture are *tillage*, " which comprehends *flax* and *flax-seed*, re- " claiming *waste lands*, feeding cattle; and the " linen being *exportable*, stamps its own value " to the kingdom.

" Let us turn the scale, and suppose that " we had a free exportation of silk and woollen " goods, instead of the produce of our land

" and

" and linen. Cool and difpaffionate reafon
" will furely fee, that we fhould have much
" more reafon to complain than we have now,
" becaufe there could be no proportion in the
" profit. England and France would ever be
" our competitors in the woollen, and the
" filk could afford but a fmall profit, becaufe
" the material is foreign and very coftly ; be-
" fides which, when could we hold a com-
" petition with the other two nations ? But
" when we add another confideration to our
" prefent latitude, that the Englifh have laid,
" not only a duty of ten per cent. upon the
" importation of German linens, thereby open-
" ing their markets to the Irifh, but alfo an
" equal bounty on the exportation of Irifh and
" Englifh linens, furely we fhould reflect upon
" thofe meafures, as living teftimonies of her
" paternal affection."

I am, fir, yours,

Y   A MERCANT.

NUMBER XVIII.

Projicit ampullas & fesquipedalia verba.

To JEOFFRY WAGSTAFFE, Efq.

SIR,

I AM too well acquainted with Doctor Lucas, to be furprifed at his effrontery, in attempting to impofe on his readers by falfe affertions, and empty declamation ; the public have always treated his productions with deferved contempt. ——The loyal inhabitants of this kingdom have perfevered in their allegiance, though every bafe and mean art has been repeatedly ufed to excite them to riot and faction.   In vain has the trumpet of fedition re-echoed from St. Audeon's Arch ;——In vain has a felfifh, difappointed junto dreffed up the dæmon of licentioufnefs, to refemble the goddefs of liberty : the cheat was too apparent, and as eafily diftinguifhed as the daubing of a fign-painter from the tints of a Titian.

The Doctor feems very angry, " that our " worthy chief magiftrate had not authority or " influence enough to keep a board of alder- " men together, *to take the important matters he* " *offered,*

" *offered, under their confideration.*"—It feems,
neither the inattention, contempt, or abhorrence of every rational and temperate man, can
damp the Doctor's noble ardour in the caufe of
faction. Neither the contemptuous fneers of
the Houfe, the recufant gates of Leinfter-place,
nor Lord Shannon's dignified filence on the
political part of a congratulatory letter, can
lower this dotard's vanity.——What curb can
reftrain a vicious horfe with a bad mouth?
then how can fhame or decency check the
innate petulance of this defpicable old man?——
He remains obftinately blind to a plain circumftance, which every one muft fee, " that
" he had really nothing material to offer ;"
or even if he had propofed any public meafure
of real utility, the turpitude of the man would
have difgraced it.

Let me now congratulate the Doctor on his
firft feelings as a parent : he " laments the
" pious fon, punifhed for the virtues of the
" father ; and the father for the virtues of the
" children." I know no where this tragic
fcene has been acted : furely this ingenuous
writer does not allude to Mr. P——n——by,
whofe political crimes he has regularly regif-
tered in the Freeman. However, the Doctor
may bid defiance to this fpecies of minifterial

vengeance; his unnatural conduct has effectually preserved his family from such compli-
cated persecution.

It is difficult to draw any conclusion from
the vague, embarrassed allegation in the sixth
paragraph of the Doctor's letter. If he means
to insinuate that any promise was made by the
Vice-roy, the plain state of the case will con-
fute his assertion.—The Quarterage-bill, like
all others, must pass through both houses of
parliament, and receive the sanction of the
council, before the Lord Lieutenant can constitutionally interfere, or recommend it to his
Majesty for the royal assent. Is it to be supposed that his Excellency would enter into
any previous engagement, or does the Doctor
alledge, that any application was made to him
by the corporation, with this view. If he
does, with what indignity does he treat his
fellow citizens, by supposing they could esteem a chief governor's patronage sufficient
security for passing any bill, before the
parliament or council had debated upon it.——
The very idea is preposterous; the inference
injurious, both to the honour of parliament,
and the character of those who presented the
bill, with the usual *complimentary address.* The
Doctor forgets that a specious shew of pro-
babililty

bability is effentially requifite, even to obtain
a momentary credit for his fcurrilous falfe-
hoods, and grofs defamation.

Perhaps this babbler will fay, " That the
" weavers petition, prefented by the Marquis
" of Kildare, was infolently and meanly re-
" fufed."—— It would have degraded government, and been difrefpectful to the city, to
have received an anonymous, unauthorifed
petition on the very day that a legal, loyal,
and proper addrefs was prefented, on the fubject of national grievances. That addrefs
was immediately tranfmitted to England, and
moft gracioufly received by his Majefty——His
Excellency paid a polite attention to the Marquis of Kildare, as a perfon of rank and
character, but could not carry his compli-
fance farther.

I fhall now reduce the Doctor's elaborate
epiftle to a few clear and diftinct points. In
a paffionate addrefs to the obftinate, and unfeeling aldermen, he thus exclaims: " Have
" they not feen, have they not felt the ge-
" neral ftagnation of the trade and manufac-
" tures of the kingdom, the confequent
" decreafe of the revenue, confeffedly brought
" on by the violent outrages of adminiftra-
" tion."———The venerable and celebrated

VOL. II. K repre-

representative of the city of Dublin, feems ignorant of the very elements of commerce: he does not yet know, that the revenue arifes from our imports, and not from our exports. The linen manufacture, our ftaple commodity, was never in a more flourifhing condition: the dreadful prorogation did not affect it. Our Weftern exports, beef, butter, pork, &c. have annually increafed. The deficency of the revenue, indeed, has furnifhed ample fcope for patriotic mifreprefentation, though it might be eafily proved that the balance of trade in our favour, is *proportionate* to this very deficiency——for the revenue arifes from our import duties, which chiefly confift of foreign luxuries;—— confequently national commerce by which I mean our export trade, may flourifh, when the revenue is at the loweft ebb. The abfurdity of the Doctor's logic and complaints, muft appear evident to the meaneft capacity. If I were to apologize to the patriot's conftituents for his folly, I fhould fay he reafons from analogy, and wifely concludes, that a dofe of futile, perplexed declamation, may prove as falutary to weak brains, as affes milk to weak lungs: thus he prefcribes and adminifters both with equal fkill, in his political and medical capacity.

" Yet

" Yet do they not fee," continues the Doctor, " the military eftablifhment augmented be- " yond all tolerable bounds." Thefe are his fentiments on that judicious parliamentary augmentation, by which the royal prerogative was reftrained, and a corps of 12000 troops provided for the defence and fecurity of the people who pay them. This public fpirited meafure, executed with the ftricteft œconomy, produced a faving of 23,385l. 15s. 8d. This was effected by the Lord Lieutenant's *innovating* on the ufual mode of iffuing pay for the in- tended argumentation, as foon as it was voted. By this means, a large non-effective fund be- came the property of the public, and was applied to the fervice of the ftate.

The reduction of the ftaff has alfo produced an annual faving of 2737l. 10s. od. Thefe regulations were adopted by a *military* Viceroy. " Can they (*i. e.* the aldermen) pretended to " be ignorant of the ftate of the national debt ? " Muft they not fee, that at Lady Day 1769, " it did not exceed 628,883l. 17s. 10d. Yet " at Lady Day 1771, it arofe to the fum of " 789,569l. 7s. 8d. *And that the arrears amount to no lefs than 1,057,151l. 15s. 7d.*"

The difference between the national debt in 1769, and 1771, was principally occafioned by

K 2

the

the increafed charge of the military eftablifhment, which was accordingly forefeen and
provided for, by a vote of credit for 100,000l.
Tho' the arrears amount to 1,054,171l. 2s. 10d.
yet if the doctor had been ingenuous, he would
have inferted the following words from the
General State of the National Accounts.

" Arrears due at Lady Day 1771, (including
" the national debt) 1,054171l. 2s. 10d.   To-
" wards which muft be applied balances and
" arrears due at Lady Day 1771, on the re-
" venue, loan duties, &c. &c. which amount
" to 264,601l. 15s. 1½d."

But the doctor, who never deviates into truth,
either ignorantly or infidioufly, points out the
arrears as a feparate article, and an additional
burthen on the kingdom. Certainly, fir, the
aldermen perceived this mean, ungenerous de-
ception (for I fuppofe your letter in the Freeman, is only a copy of the paper you laid
before them) and therefore treated you with
the contempt you deferved. " And yet do
" they not know, that regardlefs of the enor-
" mous debt contracted, the penfions, con-
" cordatums, incidents are continually in-
" creafed and multiplied upon the eftablifh-
" ment." In anfwer to this falfehood, I
fhall only obferve, that the penfions are decreafed

creafed 2700l. per annum during Lord Townfhend's adminiftration, nor is any other inci-
dental expence augmented.

I need not expatiate on the many excellent
laws which will always diftinguifh his Excell-
lency's government, particularly the Octennial
Bill. This grateful nation is indebted to L.
T. for the Abfentee Tax, nor has he ever
exerted his intereft or influence to counteract
its beneficial effects. He refufed to recommend
Lord Chief Juftice Clayton's requeft to the
king, for a nett annuity of 1000l. His conduct on this, and *fimilar* applications, is his
beft eulogium.

Happily, fir, " your rulers (as you ftyle
" the worthy aldermen) have common under-
" ftanding ;" they do not fee that the Chief
Governor meant to include the loyal city of
Dublin, " in that part of his fpeech where he
" points out different parts of this kingdom,
" as engaging in lawlefs affociations, and com-
" mitting violent outrages." Are not thofe
Proteftant fons of liberty, the Hearts of Steel,
at prefent houghing cattle, burning houfes,
and perfecuting their fellow-fubjects in the
North? Are not thofe Catholic fons of liberty,
the White Boys, in the center of the kingdom,
dragging people out of their beds, burying
K 3   them

them alive, and deftroying their property? You will anfwer perhaps, that the White Boys are not exactly in the center of the kingdom— and be fure to make a motion, and divide on this in parliament. You may modeftly move the Houfe to enter into fome fpirited refolution: for inftance, * " That any reflection on the " county of Antrim, contains an injurious " cenfure againft the county of Tyrone : that " houghing cattle, burning houfes, and fuch " trifling offences, are not *fpecifically* riots : " that the indignation of the people was " conftitutionally expreffed on the firft of " March, in College-Green : that the beating " two or three Bifhops, and menacing a few " Temporal Lords and Commoners with " death, was not a riot or breach of the " peace." Remember, always to divide on thefe important queftions. In fhort, nothing will fatisfy you, but thofe glorious days, when the common-halls fhall dictate to the throne, and mobs to parliament : when regulators fhall difarm the troops, and fwaddlers fuper- feded the clergy : when a Lucas fhall bully a Lord Mayor, and inftruct a Lord Lieutenant. —Ridiculed, expofed, and fmarting from the correction you have often received, you ftill

* Vide Journals of the Houfe.

4

have

have recourfe to that ftale expedient, of reco-
vering your confequence by preaching up fedition, and mixing with the rabble.   You
were aptly compared to a battered Shrove-
Tuefday cock, that is reftored to life and vigour by having his head plunged in a dunghill.   You difguft every reader of tafte with
your flovenly inaccuracies, your grovelling
ftyle, and obfcure tautologies, *toleruble bounds*,
fall and *downfull* of your country—the *ruins* of
liberty, &c.——You muft certainly fuppofe the
temple of liberty fituated in fome alley in
Meath-ftreet, perhaps you miftake the weavers
afylum for that facred dome; *there* you may
at laft retire, and enjoy *otium cum dignitate*, if
the hard-hearted aldermen ftill refufe you a
ftipend.

October 30th, 1771.

DIOGENES.

NUM-

NUMBER XIX.

—⸺— For our end
We muſt ſuggeſt the people, in what hatred
He ſtill hath held them, that to power he would
Have made them mules, ſilenc'd their pleaders, and
Diſproperty'd their freedoms : holding them
In human action and capacity,
Of no more ſoul, or fitneſs in the world,
Than camels in the war, who have their provender,
Only for bearing burthens, and ſore blows
For ſinking under them.

To JEOFFRY WAGSTAFFE, Eſq.

SIR,

YOU have wiſely, in my opinion, avoided
as much as poſſible, entering into any alter-
cationwith the ſupporters of thoſe two contemptible vehicles of public ſedition and private ſcan-
dal, the Freeman and Hibernian, and indeed have
left them in a great meaſure unnoticed. However,
I hope you will not object to theſe few ſtric-
tures on Brutus's letter of the 3d of this month :
he there affects to give an impartial ſtate of the
public account between the Lord Lieutenant
and the Nation, conſidered as debtor and creditor. To add weight to his reaſoning, he

copies

copies the example of the Grub-ftreet pub-
lifhers of *red and black lifts*; doubtlefs con-
ceiving, that the colours which heretofore
doomed fo many members of parliament to
eternal obloquy, or configned them to immortal fame, will carry equal conviction to the
underftanding of his credulous readers. This
dull, faftidious, lying performance, is evidently
the child of the puritanic O—l—r P—k—t,
notwithftanding the declarations in the fame
paper to the contrary; his malignant levelling
fpirit is apparent through the whole; in de-
nying it, he only copies the example of his late
coadjutor, doctor Lucas.

It is to be prefumed, that this worthy author
affumes his fignature from the factious tribune
mentioned by Shakefpeare; a man who brought
his country to the brink of deftruction, by the
perfecution of her beft and braveft citizens;—
how unlike that immortal Roman, who, from
a confcientious and ardent love of liberty,
drew his fword againft an ufurping tyrant!—
I am the laft man, Mr. Wagftaffe, that would
proftitute my pen to palllate or apologize for
the *actions* of corrupt magiftrates, who plunder
or infult my country; much lefs of a Vice-roy
who deferved that character. On the other
hand, I think it the duty of every friend to

K 5   truth,

truth, and the public weal, to oppose the turbulence of a restless faction, to detect and expose the falsehoods, insidiously calculated to poison the minds of the credulous multitude, and to check the overweaning pride of those malecontents, who cannot brook that subordinate rank in the community, which chance or nature has assigned them.——Whoever reflects seriously on the conduct and views of these *men*, will easily discern how impossible it is for the most prudent and mild government to ensure the peace and good order of society. The malignant, though contemptible libels of a Pl—k—t, may disgrace the country which was immortalized by a Walker; whilst those popular ruffians, Savage and Redmond, shall parade over the very ground, where the illustrious William marched to our salvation. Such miscreants, as *professed friends* to the prosperity of Ireland, would render every industrious inhabitant discontented with his situation, and justify the excesses of the profligate against the sober and honest part of the community, charging government (as the father of all sin) with the misery and depopulation that inevitably follows.

As *friends to the constitutions*, they exhort the juries to judge of the expediency of the law,

an

and the conduct of the legiflature who paffed it, not of the atrocioufnefs of the crime, or the proof before them ; and as *determined opponents* to military *government*, and *augmentations*, they excite and cultivate fuch a rebellious fpirit among the common people, as obliges the landed gentry, and the *northern patriots* to folicit the aid of the military, and place themfelves in fact entirely under their protection.—— Such are the patriotic confiftencies, and pious labours of Brutus Pl——k——t, and his coadjutors, however unfupported, and even condemned by the general fenfe of the nation. Indeed, I cannot recollect any county (Meath excepted), or corporate town, which has adopted his language. The general opinion and voice of this kingdom breathe nothing but a dutiful acknowledgment of the virtues and firmnefs of our truly amiable fovereign, though he is reprefented in our loyal papers as an ideot, a tyrant, a Jacobite, and a patron of Sodomites. With refpect to his fubftitute here, I fhould be at a lofs to determine his real character, were it not for thofe public teftimonials he has received from fo many counties and corporations, which have never been cancelled, as I hear, by any one authentic difavowal, during an unufual refidence of five years.

K 6   Here

Here might be the proper place to enter into a particular difcuffion with Brutus, both as to his Excellency's public and private cha-racter ; for I obferve that he is as accurate an arithmetician as Sir W——ll——m M——ne, and keeps a *pence-table* to regifter his charities ; as *thefe* are of a private nature, and belong only to the feelings of the heart, I fhall take no no-tice of them. The Lord Lieutenant's atten-tion to our public works, charter fchools, foundling hofpital, &c. is remembered by every thinking man, when the violence and felfifh fpirit of a party had drawn on the prorogation. It was a bitter difappointment to a faction, which hoped to bring every calamity on their country, to fee themfelves defeated by the kind attention and benevolence of the crown.

Let me proceed to ftate Brutus's charges, with explicit anfwers, and then prefent the candid and impartial reader with a true account of the many extenfive benefits this country has received in the quinquenium of Lord Town-fhend's adminiftrations.

Brutus's Charge.

Prorogation.

To be imputed to Mr. P. and the patriots, who paffed a ufelefs and unconftitutional vote. The parliament met the following winter,

merely

merely to tranfact the national bufinefs, in confequence of a decent and dutiful addrefs from
the city of Dublin.

Oppreffions of the veterans at Kilmainham.

An abfolute falfehood. · The contemptible
ftring of lies .on this head, can be confuted
by the teftimony of every governor of the hofpital.

Riot Act.

All counties fhould have a Riot Act, who
prefer a legal, to a mob government.

Penfions to whores and pimps.

The charge on the civil lift for penfions, is
decreafed 6cool. per annum during Lord Townfhend's adminiftration ; nor has he loaded the
eftablifhment with a fingle one for any of his
blood or relations.——An unprecedented inftance
of difinterieftednefs.

*Squandering the public money to purchafe mem-
bers of parliament.*

An abfurd falfehood.——If the charge could
be proved, why did your patriots drop their
long blazoned enquiry ?

*Obftructing the act, that the judges fhould
hold their employments, quam diu fe bene gefferint.*

The nation is obliged to Lord Townfhend
for his good intentions : he promoted and recommended this act in the ftrongeft manner.——

The

The Prime Serjeant, laſt ſeſſions, explained the true principle, *why* a clauſe was inſerted in that bill, which induced the commons to re-ject.it.

Livings to many ungodly men.

Puritanic cant and nonſenſe.

Augmentation Act.

The beſt military regulation ever adopted. ——Prerogative reſtrained, and the defence and ſecurity of the kingdom provided, for by the ſame means.

Breach of the royal promiſe, &c.

Abſolutely falſe.——The army *in* this king-dom, conſiſts of four regiments of horſe, eight of dragoons, and twenty-two regiments of foot; they all are as complete as poſſible, *allowing for deaths and deſertions.*

Sinking the Quarterage-Bill.

It is to be feared that the Lord Lieutenant has not ſo much merit on this occaſion, as is imputed to him.——Ireland is the only Proteſtant country, which does not encourageable and induſ-trious ſtrangers.   The bad policy of this inju-dicious prevention, is owing to the pitiful local jealouſies of the noiſy and monopolizing corpo-rations of a metropolis, ſinking under diſſipa-tion and faction.

The

The spirit of the Absentee-tax dispensed with.

This grateful nation is indebted to Lord Townshend for the Absentee-tax; nor has he exerted his interest or influence to counteract its beneficial effects.   He refused to recommend Lord Chief Justice Clayton's request to the King, for a nett annuity of 1000l.——His conduct on this, and similar applications, is his best eulogium.

Supporting Popery Acts.

No acts have been supported by government, but such as will conciliate the minds of dutiful, peaceable, though unfortunate subjects, at the same time that they tended to cure that evil which the Freeman so loudly complained of——a scarcity of cash.

Appointing useless surveyors.

The improvement or decline of the revenue will prove whether they are useless or not.

Preventing (or at best, not recommending) the return of Grier's and Howard's bill.

Another bold lie——The true cause of its failure was occasioned by some English creditors, who petitioned the privy council——and their objections were deemed valid.

Not encouraging trade by residing at Black Rock.

Is his Excellency to live all the summer at the Castle ?——Then why do not our patriots reside in Dublin also ? Are not levees held every
week ?

week? and is not all the cash for the maintenance of his houfhold expended in Dublin?——
Which of our patriots can fay with his Excellency, that they themfelves, or their families,
have never worn any thing but Irifh manufacture during five years?

*Difgracing the reprefentative of Majefty, by
keeping company with the diffolute and abandoned.*

I much fear his Majefty himfelf will be
more difgraced in the next papers.——Who are
thefe diffolute and abandoned?——Is it owing
to the charity of the Freemen, that they remain
in the fhade?

*By appointing men, fcarcely a degree above
ideots, to feats in the privy council.*

Are their underftandings inferior to Lord
L——th's, Lord W——ft——th's, fir W——ll——m
M——ne's or Mr. P——nf——by's?

By appointing men to the office of HighSheriffs, &c.

It is notorious that juftice is more imparti-
ally adminiftered than ever, by the appointment
of fheriffs: to maintain a ftrict impartiality in
counties, where ftrong divifions prevail, the
fheriffs are frequently nominated *alternately* from
each party.

Appointment of the five commiffioners of excife.

The judicious œconomical regulations already adopted in the revenue, prove their utility.
——In

—In a few years Mr. P——nf——by raifed the charge of collecting the revenue by incidents, &c. 45,000l. per ann. In a few months the new board have diminifhed them above 7,000l. per annum.

Commiffioners of accounts.

It is a fact, that the Lord Chancellor, and the Barons of the Exchequer, neither did, nor had leifure to examine the national accounts with accuracy and precifion.——The faving to the nation, by the eftablifhment of this board, will be confiderable, as will moft evidently appear next feffion of parliament.

And laftly, by great mifreprefentation of the whole Irifh nation.

Where did the lying author collect this ?—— It is probable, that if his Excellency, after the prorogation, had reprefented the conduct of a violent, difappointed faction, to have been the general fenfe of the kingdom, this parliament had never met again. It is evident from *that* event, that both the Chief Governor, and the Britifh cabinet, formed a very different idea, nor were they miftaken; for the fenfe of the parliament, when they met, and the fenfe of the whole nation, has proved very different from the language of the Free Prefs, and Protefting Lords, which are no more than a weak

6   and

and contemptible imitation of the feditious language of the contemptible fupporters of the
Bill of Rights, at the London Tavern.

After thus *anfwering*, I hope, in a fatisfactory
manner, every charge urged by this defpicable
writer, I fhall conclude by recapitulating thofe
effential benefits which we have received from
him.

Abolition of Lords Juftices, and of an
ariftocratic fyftem, which was a difgrace to a
free people.

The Octennial-bill——which has diffufed an
Englifh fpirit of liberty among the freeholders
of this kingdom.

The Abfentee-tax——which produces 16 or
17,000 l. a year, and faves ten times as much
to the nation, by preventing many of our nobility and gentry from refiding abroad.

	l.	s.	d.
Actual produce of it	16,000	0	0
A refident Lord Lieutenant, (per annum) ——	16,000	0	0
The bounty on linen *renewed.* This, by *experimental proof*, oc- cafions the export of 3,564,381 yards, value ——	237,625	0	0

An

An *extenſion* of the bounty
to Iriſh printed linens.

Preventing a bounty of three
half-pence a yard on all Man-
cheſter checks, which would
have operated as a bounty of
45 l. per cent. againſt our linen
manufacture.

	l.	s.	d.
Reduction of the ſtaff,	2,737	0	0
Penſions diminiſhed –	60,000	0	0

The Privilege-bill, which
has *diſobliged* ſeveral of the patriots, by ſubjecting them to
the laws of their country, and
compelling them to act like
honeſt men.

The Bankrupt-bill, which
will extend our trade, by eſta-
bliſhing confidence and credit
among our Merchants.

The Rum-bill—which will
extend to our commerce, and
increaſe the Revenue.

| | 40,000 | 0 | 0 |

A judicious parliamentary augmentation, by
which the royal prerogative was reſtrained, and
a corps of twelve thouſand troops provided for
the

the defence and fecurity of the people who pay
them. That public fpirited meafure, executed
with the ftricteft œconomy, produces a faving
of 23,3581. 15s. 8d. This was effected by
the Lord Lieutenant's *innovating* on the ufual
mode of iffuing pay for the intended augmentation as foon as it was voted. By this
means, a large non-effective fund became the
property of the public, and was applied to the
fervice of the ftate.

The appointment of more Irifh judges,
and Irifh bifhops, than any of his predeceffors.

V E R A X.

N U M B E R   XX.

Diram qui contudit Hydram,
Notaque fatali portenta labore fubegit,
Comperit invidiam fupremo fine domari.   Hor.

To Jeoffry Wagstaffe, Efq.

S I R,

YOUR correfpondent Verax, in his excellent letter of the 24th of laft month,
gave a detail at once fo ample and impartial of
Lord Townfhend's merits to this country, that
he has left little for the friends of government
to

to fupply, or for its enemies to object, on that exhaufted fubject. That paper contained fuch an enumeration of benefits conferred on Ireland within thefe laft five years, that it looked rather like a catalogue of objects to be defired, than of acquifitions already obtained, and of which we are at this moment in actual poffeffion. Were a body of the moft fanguine and requiring electors, in this fanguine and requiring age and nation, to propofe conditions of eternal vote and fuffrage to any undertaking candidate for their favour, I fuppofe the extravagance of ignorant expectation could hardly fwell out a lift of fuch conftitutional articles, as are comprifed in that fair ftate of debtor and creditor, between the prefent Governor and the people. Compare it with what was obtained for Ireland in any former period of the fame duration, nay, of three times the fame duration, and detraction herfelf will fcarce hefitate to pronounce, that this man deferves an everlafting monument in the breaft of every real friend to his country. The name of Chefterfield is ftill mentioned among us with refpect and veneration : we fay he was a wife, a temperate, and a difinterefted ruler : we hold up his example as a fatire on thofe who went before, and a model for thofe who are to come

after

after him. And why? He came to Ireland it is true at a very critical juncture: the King's title was denied, and a Pretender to his crown was advancing at the head of some furious mountaineers, to dispute it with him in his capital. The policy of government in this kingdom, at such a time, was obvious: to betray no apprehension of a revolution in England, nor to exercise unnecessary severities towards a large body of the people, whose imbecility was confirmed before, by the laws which had stripped them of the means of rendering disloyalty formidable. This was the policy, and this the merit of Lord Chesterfield. His lordship's discernment, and the season, co-operated to establish his reputation: the suavity of his manners gained him many private friends: he cultivated men of letters; and they transmitted him to posterity with the partiality inseparable from the distinguished notice with which he had honoured them. Many of his sayings are still in the mouths of his contemporaries. But it is in vain to search the public records of that æra, for any improvement of our commerce, our finances, or our constitution. However honourable and satisfactory the revision of Verax may be to the present, it requires no spirit of divination to foresee, that

it

it will be the fource of much comparative cenfure, of much difquiet and bitternefs, to the
fucceeding adminiftration : not that a fpirit of
laudable emulation will be wanting to that
worthy and amiable nobleman who is fhortly to
prefide in this kingdom, but, in truth, fo much
has been done by his predeceffor, that it is difficult to fay, what is there attainable that remains to be performed. To encreafe the revenues of a country, without adding to the burthen of its taxes ; to confirm its liberties, and
improve its conftitution, without diminution of
the royal prerogative ; at once to augment its
armies, and fecure its tranquility ; to extend
its commerce, without prejudicing the mother-
country, are objects of diftinguifhed magnitude ;
and the poffibility of fo rare a combination may
not exift again in a long feries of our unevent-
ful hiftory.

.Thefe are the veftiges which Lord Townfhend will leave behind him. By thefe will
his name be remembered, when private pique,
and perfonal animofity, are totally extinguifh-
ed : when the veil of mifreprefentation is with-
drawn from his actions ; and when the libel of
the day is buried in the duft of neglect and ob-
livion.

The

The mode of attacking his person and measures, has been hitherto, varied according to the nature of the defence, and the different genius of the assailants.

At one time, his conduct as a soldier in a former part of his life (though totally unconnected with his present situation) was the favourite theme of defamation. Every exploded calumny against the military reputation of the American general, was hauled from antiquated gazetteers and journals, to confront and embarrass the Vice-roy of Ireland. In vain were these base falsehoods crushed by authentic vouchers in your paper, they crawled again and again before the public thro' long columns of chronicles and registers, and some purpose was answered; while the giddy multitude, always disposed to judge unfavourably of their superiors, and who have neither heads nor tempers to examine both sides of a question, could be persuaded that little worthy was to be expected from the statesman, when nothing meritorious had been performed by the officer. At another time, when notoriety made it impossible to deny the public acts of his government, the acts indeed were at last admitted, but the attainment was ascribed to some other influence; and while parliament was expressing the thanks

of

of the nation by votes and addresses to Lord Townshend, Grub-street tuned pæans and gratulations to a Shelbourne, a Hertford, or to some minister on the other side, who might perhaps wish well to the interests of Ireland, but in these instances had no more right to our acknowledgments, than the Roman Pontiff has to the homage of his grace of Canterbury.

But the last resource of these baffled controvertists is still more extraordinary. Say these ingenious gentlemen, take away the Limitation Act, Bounty on Irish Linen, Absentee-tax, Rum-bill, and the like, and where is the pre-eminence of Lord Townshend's administration ? It sinks at once to a level with the most corrupt or insignificant that ever went before it. If we admit the premises, we have certainly no right to quarrel with the conclusion : nay it will be but just to allow these miserable sophisters all the advantages they can hope to derive from such a candid state of the argument, since their *petitio principii* shews at once the desperate state of their cause, and the streights to which they are reduced both as logicians and incendiaries. I am not at a loss to discover from whence they have borrowed this species of casuistry. The prototype of their sentence on the administration of his Excel-

lency, is to be found in the taylor's judgment,
who being asked what he thought of the prospect from Richmond-hill, after mature deliberation, pronounced gravely, that *if the trees
and the water were away*, it would be nothing
extraordinary.

As this is probably the last time I shall ever
trouble your readers with my sentiments on
matters of a public nature, I cannot lay down
my pen, without taking some notice of a writer who has thrust himself into observation, not
so much by the merit, as by the length and
frequency of his labours. A mirror which reflects nothing that can displease or mortify, is
the last into which a man should look, who
wishes to see his imperfections, that he may
amend them: and it is evident, the self-satisfied Brutus, has hitherto contemplated himself
in no other. That which I mean to hold up
to him, is of a different nature, it will give
him back his features neither softened nor distorted.

Assertions without facts to support them;
epithets taken up at random from the refuse of
diction; meagre sentiments and self-evident propositions, introduced with an air of triumphant
discovery; personality and lying, without pungency or invention; wandering allusions, com-

parisons

parifons where there is no circumftance of fimilitude, rhapfodies at once delirious and heavy, fpiritlefs apoftrophes, jumbled metaphors; falfe rhetoric, and falfe Englifh, are the characteriftics of a performance, which the complacent fatisfaction of its author has thought worthy of a feparate publication, and which he modeftly tells us, in fome puffing paragraphs of his own framing, are equal in point of compofition to the letters of Junius. He has, however, qualified this extravagant eulogium, by allowing that fomething is to be abated from the merit of Brutus, in confideration of the different rank of the fubjects : by which it is to be fuppofed, he means their different importance ; or, in other words, that it is more important to libel his Majefty, than his reprefentative ; more daring to write treafon, than fcurrility ; and a more arduous undertaking to miflead the hot-brained populace of London, than to inflame the ragged rabble of the Coombe and Meath-ftreet.——Some qualities of the heart, he may be allowed to poffefs, in common with that celebrated partizan of Englifh oppofition ; and in their fituations, there may, perhaps, be fomething fimilar : it is plain indeed, that they are both exafperated, vindictive, and feditious : but the parallel can go no

farther.

farther.— Junius has an absolute dominion over his subject, and shews equal art in what he conceals from the public, and in what he divulges.   He often throws false lights on his canvas, but his colouring is always vivid. Though we detect his fallacies, we must admire his ingenuity; and while we read his lively invectives, it is impossible not to wish, that so much energy and acuteness of genius, had been called out in the support of a better cause, and that his zeal had been tempered by more sober and constitutional principles : but this poor drudge of a baffled faction, scarce deserves the lowest rank in the files of Grub-street. Destitute of every requisite to form an able advocate, and so far from possessing the powers of enforcing or illustration, he is not master of precision enough even to state intelligibly the pretended grievances of his party ; so that his cause, his patrons, and his antagonist, come out of his hands, pretty much as he found them ; the first, indeed, somewhat weakened by his incapacity ; the second, unadorned by his panegyric ; and the last, uninjured by his invectives.

I am, sir, your humble servant,

Z   AN OCCASIONAL WRITER.

NUMBER XXI.

Provoco ad populum.

THE writers on the fide of government have been accuftomed to the appellation of hirelings and mercenaries; they have been accufed of uttering their notions on national bufinefs, not from principle, but for pay. It has been prophefied of them, that when it was no longer their intereft to defend the meafures of their patron, they would leave him to the indignation of the people; or, perhaps, unite with thofe who had reviled him moft bitterly; and, by a public defertion of their opinions, make the beft apology in their power for having entertained them.

The conduct of thefe gentlemen has given a practical refutation to this fcurrilous conjecture:

Domus hâc nec purior ulla eft,
Nec magis his aliena mal.s.

Had they engaged in the fupport of adminiftration, from the fame motives with thofe who wifh to render it odious, the going down of Lord Townfhend's fun would have chilled

their

their zeal in his service; and the first notification of a successor would have benumbed their faculties. Interest indeed, is for ever fluctuating; subject to ague fits and vicissitudes, hot and cold, high and low, as the political barometer falls or rises; but principle knows no such changes: self-centered, it is superior to external accidents; independent of every thing but itself, it acts steadily, consistently, and openly. The support of a public-spirited administration, is an employment worthy of any man's leisure and abilities, and it has lately devolved on persons, who have never published any opinion, which they have not been able to defend by the authority of the most approved authors; nor have they ever offered to impose a measure on the ignorance, or credulity of their countrymen, but have given the whole of their information without disguise, reserve, or false colouring; appealing to the incontestible evidence of facts, and submitting every circumstance to the judgment of their readers. If notions illiberal and unconstitutional, have at any time crept into the publications supposed to be sanctioned by government, a disavowal has immediately followed; and the only tolerable answer which has yet appeared to the erroneous sentiments, expressed against the Diffenters of this kingdom, (in a late Batchelor) is to be found in a paper, which almost trod upon its heels, under the signature of Timoleon. Had such a refutation appeared from the popular press, what encomiums should we not have heard on the fagacity and information of the author? What triumph for the victory? What insults over the vanquished?

Lord Townshend has been repeatedly accused of profusion in the management of the public money, and of parsimony in that of his own. The reverse of this injurious charge is nigher the truth. After five years administration, amidst the conflict of factions, the fublety of intrigue, and the violence of party-rage; at a period, when the venal and corrupt estimate their votes by the necessity of government, and suppose their own want of principle justified by that very necessity.——Such an epoch in our politics, seems ill calculated for the reform of abuses, and the introduction of wife and judicious regulations into every branch of our civil and military establishments. To enter into a minute discussion on these heads, would exceed the limits of my paper. A Chief Governor is entitled to our just and merited eulogiems, who is neither to be cajoled by flat-

tery,

fery, or intimidated by menaces, to deviate from that line of duty, which his own situation and the public good prescribe; and who, by the firmness, the rectitude, and disinterestedness of his conduct, introduces and establishes a system of œconomy, pregnant with national benefits; and checks a system of jobbing, pregnant with national disgrace.

The annual savings will appear extraordinary, and unprecedented; especially, if the state of our establishments at the conclusion of Lord Townshend's administration, is contrasted with that of his predecessors at the same period.—— I shall, therefore, submit the following abstract to the candour and impartiality of the public.

Amount of the Civil Establishments, at the commencement of the administrations of the following Lord Lieutenants.

	£.		
1763. April 3d. Earl of Hallifax,	107,754	4	7
Increase in his administration,	8,707	4	5
1763. April 27th. E. of Northumberland,	116,461	9	0
Increase in his administration,	11,244	16	2½
1765. Aug. 7th. Earl of Hertford, —	127,706	5	2½
Increase in his administration,	1,547	5	7
1766. Oct. 6th. Earl of Bristol, —	129,253	10	9½
Increase in his administration,	8,500	0	0

1767: Aug. 19. Lord Townshend, — £. 137,753 10 9½
    Amount, 30th of September, 1772, 134,053 0 2½
          which his own and

       : Decrease, — £. 3,695 10 6½

In Aug. 1767, the pensions amounted to 86,741 7 6
The 30th of September, 1772, — 76,669 17 6

        Decrease, — £. 10,131 10 0

'Since that time, 'King's letters have come
over for granting above five thousand pounds
in pensions;—still there is an annual saving
of 5000 l. on this invidious article.

MILITARY ESTABLISHMENTS.
The half-pay in August, 1767, — £. 36,481 7 4½
September 30th, 1772, — — 26,606 4 4½

      'Annual decrease, — £. 9,875 3 0½

I should not omit observing, that the half-
pay list, like the *Persian satellites*, was *formerly*
reckoned immortal, as the officers were con-
stantly allowed to sell; and Mr. P——ns——by
also took care to convert it into a *civil* list,
and prostituted *that* public bounty for the support of the deserving soldier, in pensions to his
creatures and dependents. The shameful mis-
application of this fund, was prevented by Lord
Townshend; and no solicitations, or impor-
tunities from any quarter, could ever induce
him to swerve from his determined resolution
on this important object.

                    The

The reduction of the staff has produced
  an annual saving of — — £. 2,737 0 0
In the ordnance, — — —   579 8 4

	Revenue Establishment, ending	Revenue Incidents.
Lady Day 1770,	£. 82,787 15 10	£. 30,647 12 3
1772,	80,720 11 2	26,003 4 3

Decrease,   — £. 2,067 4 5   £. 4,644 8 0
Incidents,   —   4,644 8 0

Total decrease,   £. 6,711 12 5

Which is more than the additional expence, contracted by the division of the boards.

The receipt of the revenue, since the 25th of March, has been more than in the same period of the preceding by 55,000 l. from which 20,000 l. may be deducted for the additional duty on rum.——Yet there will still remain 35,000 l. (a sum nearly equal to one year's interest of our whole debt) *increase* in half a year.

I have studiously confined myself, in this concluding essay on Lord Townshend's government, to particular points of his ministerial conduct: to expatiate on the public acts of his administration, is now become an unnecessary, and superfluous labour. The improvement of our constitution, the extension of our commerce, the encrease of our revenue, and

the

the bounty on our linens, are now become the themes of common conversation; and the fuccefsful exertion of his Excellency's influence, in obtaining them, are no longer difputed. They are acknowledged, even in the productions of the Free Prefs; and authenticated in heterogeneous effufions of invective and panegyric.

In the difpofal of all military commiffions, and civil offices, his Lordfhip's integrity, and that of his fecretaries, have never been impeached, or even fufpected;——the *private douceurs* of office, and every fpecies of corruption, have been banifhed from thefe departments. Lord Townfhend's name and memory, will be revered with gratitude by a generous, a difcerning, and an affectionate people. The momentary, and tranfient breath of envy, which now obfcures, will then add new luftre to his reputation. Order, regularity, and œconomy, are confpicuous in every branch of our finances and revenue; and the fame benign public fpirit has given us laws, which will render us a rich and flourifhing nation. Lord Townfhend's adminiftration has been treated like one of thofe ancient temples, which is admired by every perfon of tafte and judgment, for the fimplicity of it's architecture, and elegant correfpondence

of

of its decorations ; yet the mere vulgar, un-
moved by its symmetry and beautiful propor-
tions, render its arcades, and porticoes, a dif-
gusting scene of defilement and pollution.

Z

Y.

F I N I S.

www.ingramcontent.com/pod-product-compliance
Lightning Source LLC
Chambersburg PA
CBHW030316270326
41926CB00010B/1385